Finding Gender Equality in the Women, Peace, and Security Agenda

Feminist Studies on Peace, Justice, and Violence

Series Editors: Tiina Vaittinen, Shweta Singh, and
Catia C. Confortini

This series provides a forum for the expanding feminist scholarship on questions of justice, peace, and violence, beyond the war/peace dichotomy. It integrates and pushes forward existing feminist contributions to the field of peace research, thus reinvigorating the trans-disciplinary traditions of both peace research and feminism. We publish monographs and carefully edited volumes that utilise feminist critical methodologies to shed light on gendered and sexualised violence and injustice in different empirical contexts, with the explicit normative aim of finding ways to lessen the violence and increase justice in the world. Feminists with interests in the study of direct violence (e.g., feminist security studies and feminist work on interpersonal violence), structural violence (e.g., racism and anti-racism, migration and mobility, care, and global health), epistemic peace, and justice (e.g., feminist postcolonial/decolonial and indigenous approaches to peacebuilding, intersectional and transnational analyses of justice, activist/scholar methodologies, feminist approaches to mediation, and conflict transformation) will find an intellectual home in a transdisciplinary series with broad normative dimensions – the feminist-informed inquiry into possibilities for a more just and peaceful world.

Titles in the Series:

Gender, Global Health, and Violence: Feminist Perspectives on Peace and Disease
Edited by Tiina Vaittinen and Catia C. Confortini

Banning the Bomb, Smashing the Patriarchy
By Ray Acheson

*Finding Gender Equality in the Women, Peace, and Security Agenda: From Global
Promises to National Accountability*
By Barbara K. Trojanowska

Finding Gender Equality in the Women, Peace, and Security Agenda

From Global Promises to National Accountability

By Barbara K. Trojanowska

Foreword by Cynthia Enloe

ROWMAN & LITTLEFIELD

Lanham • Boulder • New York • London

Published by Rowman & Littlefield
An imprint of The Rowman & Littlefield Publishing Group, Inc.
4501 Forbes Boulevard, Suite 200, Lanham, Maryland 20706
www.rowman.com

86-90 Paul Street, London EC2A 4NE

British Library Cataloguing in Publication Information Available

Library of Congress Cataloging-in-Publication Data

Names: Trojanowska, Barbara K., author.
Title: Finding gender equality in the women, peace, and security agenda : a roadmap from global promises to national accountability / by Barbara K. Trojanowska; foreword by Cynthia Enloe.
Description: Lanham : Rowman & Littlefield, [2022] | Series: Feminist studies on peace, justice, and violence | Includes bibliographical references and index. | Summary: "This book explores the trajectory of gender equality in institutions' engagement with the Women, Peace, and Security agenda at the intersection of global, regional, and national governance, shedding light on opportunities and challenges for a meaningful change in peace and security"— Provided by publisher.
Identifiers: LCCN 2021055966 (print) | LCCN 2021055967 (ebook) | ISBN 9781538159088 (cloth ; alk. paper) | ISBN 9781538168530 (paperback) | ISBN 9781538159095 (ebook)
Subjects: LCSH: Women in peace-building. | Women and peace. | Women—Violence against. | Sex discrimination against women. | Security, International.
Classification: LCC JZ5578 .T76 2022 (print) | LCC JZ5578 (ebook) | DDC 303.6/6082—dc23/eng/20220124
LC record available at https://lccn.loc.gov/2021055966
LC ebook record available at https://lccn.loc.gov/2021055967

That's the end goal: if we succeed with the implementation of the Women, Peace, and Security agenda as it is laid out in the resolutions, the end goal will be gender equality.

—United Nations, interview

Contents

Foreword

Cynthia Enloe

Patriarchy learns. Those many men and fewer women who see themselves as the beneficiaries of patriarchy sometimes may be slow. They occasionally may be clumsily transparent. But they do learn. They learn over time how to craft tactics and strategies to ensure patriarchy's sustainability—locally, nationally, and internationally.

That is why feminists and their allies have had to stay wide awake, energetic, and organized for more than two decades after achieving their breakthrough victory: the UN Security Council's (surprising) passage of the historic Resolution 1325 on Women, Peace, and Security.

Barbara K. Trojanowska reveals here in telling detail why and how government officials and UN agency senior staff members have resisted the full and meaningful implementation of UNSCR 1325. Reading these chapters has made me acutely aware of my own previously lazy tendency to skip over all the political wheelings and dealings between the initial passage and today's efforts. Absorbing her empirical research findings has made me realize that we all have to pay attention to every step along the way, between 2000 and 2021. Each of these steps—in New York and in capitals around the world—has been infused with its own drama, the perpetual tug between patriarchal resistance and feminist persistence.

For instance, I learned here that the very phrase *gender equality* did not start to appear in follow-up Security Council resolutions (drafted by wide-awake feminists active in civil society UN monitoring groups) until almost a decade after the original passage of UNSCR 1325. *Gender equality* was shoe-horned into these later Security Council resolutions precisely because UN member state officials and like-minded UN agency senior staff members had been sustaining masculinized privilege by going about their business acting as if UNSCR 1325 did not require them to pursue gender equality, did not commit them to dismantle patriarchy's machinery.

The Philippines and Australia share center stage here with New York's UN headquarters. This is among Trojanowska's key analytical innovations. She focuses her attention on particular governments' sometimes committed, too often ineffective, efforts to implement UNSCR 1325. Making security experts—feminist and nonfeminist—working not only in New York, but also in Manila, Canberra, and Melbourne, her key informants gives this study a genuinely global frame. It reminded me not to privilege the Security Council as a site of research, but to direct my feminist curiosity also to UN member states' diverse actors.

These state officials' own shifting political landscapes, their own broad or narrow self-interested understandings of *security* and *women's empowerment*, have been crucial in how UNSCR 1325 has been implemented. They have shaped, often diluted, the efforts to drain peacekeeping and peacebuilding processes of their patriarchal tendencies.

Barbara K. Trojanowska is a forward-looking feminist analyst. She is showing us here how our paying close analytical attention to the recent past can equip us to chart a more genuinely peaceful, necessarily less patriarchal, future.

Acknowledgments

The idea of this book has been possible because of three women. My mother, Ewa Trojanowska, instilled in me determination, optimism, and enthusiasm for the work I do. My doctoral supervisor and longtime mentor, Associate Professor Katrina Lee-Koo, endowed me with research acumen, showing with her example how to conduct rigorous research on confronting societal problems with passion, compassion, and humility. An outstanding feminist scholar and activist, Professor Cynthia Cockburn, who passed away around the time I started the work on this book, inspired my empirically driven project searching for transformative politics with her research and advocacy.

I am incredibly grateful to Professor Cynthia Enloe, who wrote the "Foreword" to this book. Her feminist scholarship has accompanied each step of my writing. I am deeply honored and humbled by her contribution.

The editors of Rowman & Littlefield International's book series on *Feminist Studies on Peace, Justice, and Violence* nurtured this project from its early days. Associate Professor Catia Cecilia Confortini, Dr. Tiina Vaittinen, and Dr. Shweta Singh challenged me to rethink key concepts, push boundaries, and take full advantage of my interdisciplinary background, intersectional identity, and international experience. I extend my thanks to the commissioning editors at Rowman & Littlefield International, including Dhara Snowden, Rebecca Anastasi, Michael Kerns, and especially Elizabeth Von Buhr and Madeline Kogler, who moved this book smoothly from manuscript to production. I also have to thank the anonymous reviewers for their helpful feedback and Vishakha Amitabh Hoskote for copyediting the manuscript.

Colleagues and friends in feminist international relations and in gender studies supported my research in various ways. I am indebted to Dr. Ava Patricia Avila, Dr. Yasmin Chilmeran, Dr. Sam Cook, Professor Sara Davies, Dr. David Duriesmith, Dr. Sri Wiyanti Eddyno, Dr. Karla Eliott, Dr. Samanthi

Gunawardana, Dr. Jenny Hedström, Dr. Melissa Johnston, Dr. Maria Koleth, Professor JaneMaree Maher, Dr. Anuradha Mundkur, Dr. Lesley Pruitt, Nina Serova, Professor Laura Shepherd, Professor Aisling Swaine, Dr. Maria Tanyag, Professor Jacqui True, and Jennifer Wittwer for their inputs into my research and their encouragement. My thanks also go to the Monash Gender, Peace and Security Centre, which provided the institutional home to my doctoral research. I would also like to note that part of chapter 4 previously appeared in the article cited and is printed here with permission: Trojanowska, B. K. (2019). Norm negotiation in the Australian government's implementation of UNSCR 1325. Australian Journal of International Affairs, 73(1), 29–44. doi:10.1080/10357718.2018.1548560.

My partner, Jonathan, offered unconditional support and patience in the final stages of writing this book, including days of free labor, while my father, Włodzimierz Trojanowski, encouraged my endeavors over the years.

I am deeply grateful to each and every person who participated in my research. I had a remarkable opportunity to travel to conduct my field research and interview nearly seventy Women, Peace, and Security specialists in multiple locations. They generously shared their expertise, insights, and time. Their work has continued to galvanize my research.

In our own ways, we all work toward this elusive goal of gender equality.

Preface

Over two decades ago, the United Nations Security Council Resolution 1325 on Women, Peace, and Security (WPS) marked the first high-level recognition of the importance of gender equality to peace and security. It did so through highlighting women's *voices* in conflict prevention, conflict resolution, and post-conflict peacebuilding, and women's *experiences* of armed conflict and insecurity. To be sure, much progress has been achieved since 2000. The participation of women in peace processes, and in peace and security efforts more broadly, has been endorsed by governments, key international and regional organizations, civil society, and militaries worldwide. Gender analysis has become an important tool in the planning and conduct of peacekeeping operations, and gender markers have been considered in relief and recovery programs in post-conflict situations. Sexual violence has been acknowledged as not only an atrocious crime and violation against human rights but also an effective weapon of war and has been addressed as such by international frameworks. Most recently, gender-based violence during COVID-19 has been hailed "the shadow pandemic" by the United Nations. All of this suggests that gender equality has become an integral part of the global peace and security discourse. Yet much more needs to be done to ensure this discourse translates into a real-life and sustainable change that supports equality and justice for all.

This interdisciplinary book has arisen from my long-standing interest in understanding how far and in what ways the WPS agenda can support the political struggle for gender equality. This interest emerged from my observations—both as a practitioner, formerly working for the Norwegian Peace Council in Oslo and the PeaceWomen Program in New York, and subsequently as a researcher at the Monash Gender, Peace, and Security Centre in Melbourne—that gender equality remained a marginalized or mostly rhetorical goal in the context of the WPS agenda, while objectives such as global stability and sustainable development continued to be prioritized by the peace and security sector and actors. The UN Security Council's High-Level Review of Women, Peace, and Security, which I had the privilege to attend in New York in 2015, was perceived by many, myself included, as a shift toward a greater emphasis on political issues of gender equality. And yet in the following years, the lack of agreement regarding the remit of the WPS agenda and the place of gender equality within it has been particularly evident, with the Security Council passing in 2019 its first WPS resolution which was not unanimously supported by its members. This was followed by an even more contentious resolution put to vote on the twentieth anniversary of the WPS agenda, which was considered by the majority of the Security Council's members a dangerous setback for the progress of the previous two decades, and therefore failed to pass.

While change has been undeniably taking place, it has not been linear, and signs of progress have occurred alongside resistance to gender equality in peace and security. As we have come this far, gender equality has proven to be a moving target and a process rather than an end goal of the WPS agenda that can be achieved once and for all. Driven by the empirics, the present book offers a systematic take on key gender equality debates and tensions within the WPS agenda. These dynamics are located at the intersection of the global, regional, and national governance, where the complexity of the pursuit of gender equality has been pronounced and entangled with competing political and institutional priorities. By looking back at the dilemmas of gender equality policymaking and their paradoxical effects in conflict and post-conflict situations, the book also looks forward to the third decade of the WPS agenda and the long-term impact of the agenda on the struggle for gender equality in peace and security.

Introduction

The Goal of Gender Equality in Peace and Security

Gender equality has been endorsed by the United Nations (UN), other international and regional organizations, governments, and civil society groups all over the globe as a key policy goal in the contemporary world. But the rhetoric around the importance of gender equality has not always matched the reality, and this has been particularly evident for some sectors where policy and institutional developments have been slower. While progress has been achieved across multiple policy areas over the most recent decades, some have remained deeply resistant to the integration of gender equality concerns.

This interdisciplinary book explores how the goal of gender equality operates in arguably the most masculinist area of politics: peace and security. While no unified understanding of gender equality or globally accepted strategy to achieve it has emerged throughout my empirically driven research, the book investigates how the meaning and purpose of gender equality has been subject to change in the policy and practice of the UN's Women, Peace, and Security (WPS) agenda, and to what effect. It does so through the analysis of gender equality in nested case studies located at multiple levels: the UN Security Council at the global level (chapter 1), the Association of Southeast Asian Nations and the Pacific Islands Forum at the regional level (chapter 2), and the governments of the Philippines and Australia at the national level (chapters 3 and 4).

The WPS agenda was originally adopted by the UN Security Council in 2000 following decades of targeted advocacy by transnational women's networks and feminist activists and researchers across the globe, most importantly in conflict-affected countries. These actors advocated for the peace and security sector, traditionally governed by male-dominated institutions and motivated by male-defined interests, to consider the role of women in conflict early warning, peace processes, peacekeeping, and peacebuilding, and to

1

take into account the gender-differentiated impact of conflict on women. The objectives around amplifying women's *voices* in peace and security processes and recognizing women's *experiences* of conflict and insecurity provided the blueprint for my understanding of gender equality in the WPS agenda.

Based on field research, interviews with key WPS stakeholders, and policy analysis, I subsequently developed a framework of gender equality in peace and security. This framework delves into how far and in what ways women's voices and experiences have been considered in the implementation of the WPS agenda, and what has been the impact of it from the global to the local (and back). Specifically, I singled out three dominant approaches that I came to call "paradigms of gender equality" as they derive from the pillars of the UN system (i.e., security, development, and human rights) that provided important ramifications for how gender equality would be envisaged and sought.

The security paradigm of gender equality calls for women's participation in police and military roles, and for improving the protection of women (and often children) from conflict-related sexual violence, by and large in contexts where such violence is deployed strategically and weaponized to terrorize affected populations. *The development paradigm of gender equality* advocates for women's participation in peace processes (often in informal roles) and peacebuilding initiatives (often at the community level), and for effective response to women's recovery needs in post-conflict, be they social, economic, or related to health. *The human rights paradigm of gender equality* promotes women's participation across the board and with no exclusions, especially participation in formal decision-making processes and positions of influence and power, as well as protection of women, men, and others from all forms of gender-based violence, whether physical or structural, across conflict and peace.

The three paradigms of gender equality have driven the policy and practice of the WPS agenda in the case studies, even though the distinction between them has not always been clear-cut. While typically coexisting, tensions and sometimes even a tug of war for dominance between the paradigms have been evident in the implementation of the WPS agenda by the UN Security Council, by the Association of Southeast Asian Nations and the Pacific Islands Forum, and by the governments of the Philippines and Australia. These tensions have been entrenched in preexisting policy environments and gender equality and security politics as well as institutional (and sometimes personal) preferences of interviewed UN, government, and civil society experts who lead the implementation of the WPS agenda in their respective contexts. Furthermore, these tensions have been exacerbated by the interplay of the goal of gender equality with political priorities identified at the global, regional, and national levels, response to COVID-19 being one of them, and with the past and present interactions with the UN system.

Through the empirical chapters of this book, I aim to establish that each paradigm has produced significant opportunities, challenges, and risks for the political struggle for gender equality. This interrogation elucidates subtleties at the heart of these policy paradigms and how they encapsulate key dilemmas—old and new—of gender equality policymaking. The multilevel analysis further exposes how the progress on gender equality (or lack thereof) has been deeply interconnected with competing interests of key stakeholders and ever-changing political landscapes. In doing so, the book provides new insights into gender equality politics at the juncture of the global and the local.

This introductory chapter sets the stage for the interrogation of gender equality as a goal of the WPS agenda at the global, regional, and national levels. Using the body of gender studies literature, I start with the outline of traditional frameworks of gender equality as well as tenets and dilemmas of gender equality policymaking. Thereafter, I trace the process by which the goal of gender equality entered the masculinist field of peace and security with the inception of the WPS agenda, engaging with international relations scholarship. Key objectives of the WPS agenda and how they relate to gender equality are explored subsequently, including the possibilities and limitations of a transformative change, and this leads to the introduction of the paradigms of gender equality. The tensions that arise in the implementation of these paradigms at the intersection of the global and the local are described in the overview of the book. This chapter ends with a discussion of the interview and documentary data utilized in the book, highlighting the benefits of feminist grounded methodology that gives primacy to the empirics and is guided by the approach of "feminist curiosity."

DILEMMAS OF GENDER EQUALITY POLICYMAKING

Gender equality is one of the most important incentives that drive feminist struggles. Simultaneously, it is one of the most problematic concepts in feminist research and one of the most troublesome objectives in policymaking (Hesse-Biber 2012; Ackerly and True 2008; 2010; Lee-Koo 2017). Even though gender equality is more and more often put forward as a goal of policies and programs, researchers aptly pointed out that "it does not necessarily follow that the same social vision accompanies the invocation of this term" (Bacchi and Eveline 2010, 2). Approaches to gender equality are multiple and diverse, both in theory and in practice (e.g., Squires 2007; 2013;

Lombardo et al. 2009; 2010; Bacchi and Eveline 2010; Walby et al. 2012; Verloo 2018; Walby 2005).

In the following, I outline key frameworks that have been prominent in gender equality policymaking. Traditionally, they range from equal opportunities, through equal outcomes, to gender mainstreaming, and bring forth theoretically distinct notions of gender equality emphasizing sameness, difference, or gender relations respectively. The analysis of these frameworks, their interconnectedness, and contradictions leads me to a conclusion that gender equality is an open concept and an unfixed policy goal that can be filled with a variety of meanings and pursued in distinct ways that serve specific interests, actors, and agendas. In offering a critical review of the frameworks of gender equality, I therefore point to the commonplace dilemmas and risks associated with gender equality policymaking, such as assimilation, essentialism, and co-optation, as well as to an increasingly important perspective of intersectionality.

Until the mid-1990s, the frameworks of equal opportunities and equal outcomes dominated equality debates (Kantola and Squires 2010; Phillips 1999; 2004; Benschop and Verloo 2006; Skjeie and Teigen 2005). Equal opportunities (or parallel approaches concerned with equal treatment before the law or formal gender equality) typically rest on the idea of sameness, whereby women and men are conceived to be inherently the same and therefore should enjoy the same access to opportunity. Driven by the strategy of "inclusion" (Squires 2007), equal opportunities are pursued through policies and programs targeted at removing any discriminatory barriers for women (or other underprivileged groups) that are in place, obstructing women's access to opportunities (Cockburn 1989). These barriers have historically prevented women from exercising political participation, leadership roles, and positions of power and influence, or from accessing certain forms of employment that were envisaged for men.

By contrast, equal outcomes (or parallel approaches focused on empowerment or advancement of women, gender equity, or substantive gender equality) aim to ensure a fair distribution of rewards (Cockburn 1989). Guided by the strategy of "reversal" (Squires 2007), the framework of equal outcomes highlights difference and points to the distinct socio-reproductive roles of women and men that have been linked to different socioeconomic outcomes. Consequently, the framework of equal outcomes calls for this difference to be considered in policies and programs that may entail the introduction of positive discrimination or affirmative action. Such special programs aim to offer a corrective to the existing inequalities. A flagship initiative is the system of gender quotas that reserves a proportion of seats for women in national assemblies and in other decision-making bodies where women have been historically underrepresented (Squires 2007), with a view to achieve greater gender balance (e.g., Krook 2006).

While influential, the frameworks of equal opportunities and equal outcomes have been criticized for fundamentally failing to challenge the status quo. Cockburn (1989, 217) maintained that approaches driven by equal opportunities and outcomes seek to "give disadvantaged groups a boost up the ladder, while leaving the structure of that ladder and the disadvantage it entails just as before." Simultaneously, equal opportunities and equal outcomes inadvertently strengthen the underlying presumption that "women can only gain equality with men if they are able to perform to the standards set by men" (Walby 2005, 326). In doing so, the frameworks of equal opportunities and equal outcomes, and the strategies of inclusion and reversal that they propagate, invoke some of the major risks associated with gender equality policymaking: assimilation and essentialism (Squires 2007). The former refers to a process and outcome by which women are "being integrated into existing (male-defined) institutions, which remain unaltered by their presence," whereas in the latter "specific identities and interests [are] being attributed to women, thereby perpetuating common sense notions of natural sex difference" (Squires 2007, 9). At times strategically useful, assimilation and essentialism are among major obstacles to gender equality because they are founded on ideas that support preexisting structures and power dynamics (Squires 2007). Even though initiatives driven by equal opportunities and equal outcomes may be a first and sometimes necessary step toward greater gender awareness in institutions that historically resisted such concerns (Benschop and Verloo 2006), only approaches that attend to the deeper structures of inequality involve "a project of transformation" (Cockburn 1989, 218). According to Cockburn (1989, 218–19), a more transformative approach "tackles power itself" and "brings into view the nature and purpose of institutions and the processes by which the power of some groups over others in institutions is built and renewed."

The promise to examine processes and practices that produce gender inequalities in different institutional settings was offered by the framework of gender mainstreaming. Since its emergence in the mid-1990s, gender mainstreaming has been an increasingly popular form of gender equality initiatives (Bacchi and Eveline 2010, 1–2; True 2010; Squires 2007; Walby 2005). Researchers described gender mainstreaming as "more comprehensive than equal opportunity policies, which focus on increasing women's access to existing organisations" and simultaneously "more transformative than positive action policies, which aim (simply) to increase the numbers of women in certain jobs or positions of influence" (Bacchi and Eveline 2010, 2). Gender mainstreaming was supposed to permeate every part of a given institution, with a view to address the needs of disadvantaged or marginalized groups and become "gender-inclusive and gender-sensitive" on the whole (Bacchi and Eveline 2010, 1–2).

Conceived as "a process to promote gender equality" (Walby 2005, 321), the purpose of gender mainstreaming is two-fold: to ensure a more systematic integration of a gender perspective in policies and planning at all levels, and to use gender analysis to assess the gender impact of these processes (Squires 2007). In doing so, gender mainstreaming draws on the notion of gender equality that highlights gender relations. That is, gender mainstreaming takes into account how the current and historical power imbalances between women and men have shaped and have been shaped by gender inequalities and sustained the subordination of women as a result. By focusing on processes and institutional structures that have produced inequalities, gender mainstreaming is driven by a strategy of "displacement" and "aims to transform the norms and institutions themselves" such that they become more gender equal (Squires 2007, 9).

Feminist advocates turned to gender mainstreaming in response to the shortcomings of frameworks of equal opportunities and equal outcomes (Bacchi and Eveline 2010; Squires 2007; Walby 2005). However, gender mainstreaming has also proven to have its challenges. Pointing to the effectiveness and impact of political processes, gender mainstreaming entails the risk of co-optation, whereby gender equality is no longer the primary goal of a given policy or program (True 2010). Rather, it is turned into a means to progress other objectives, often operational in nature, many of which are only weakly related to gender equality. In such contexts, gender mainstreaming serves the existing institutional structures and power dynamics, instead of transforming them.

The pursuit of gender equality has been further complicated by the growing concern with "diversity" and the complex relationship between gender equality and other inequalities, conventionally pertaining to class, race, and sexuality (Squires 2007, 16; Walby et al. 2012). The frameworks of equal opportunities and equal outcomes have not paid enough attention to "the diverse faces of disadvantage" (Cockburn 1989, 216), but gender mainstreaming has similarly prioritized gender inequality over other forms of discrimination or oppression. This critique is particularly identified in literature on intersectionality (e.g., Crenshaw 1991; McCall 2005; MacKinnon 2013). The perspective of intersectionality challenges "single strand" or "single axis" approaches that attend to only one form of inequality. Intersectional approaches, by contrast, are designed to tackle multiple inequalities and to challenge discrimination on the grounds of class and socioeconomic status, race/ethnicity, indigeneity and migration status, sexuality, ability, and age. By the same token, intersectional approaches recognize the interdependence of different forms of inequality, demonstrating that they are not only mutually reinforcing but also co-constituting (see also Kantola and Squires 2010). In other words, the experience of gender inequality cannot be fully understood in isolation from other intersecting inequalities.

In light of the many dilemmas embedded in gender equality policymaking, neither feminist scholars nor advocates have agreed on how to frame or attain this policy goal (Lombardo et al. 2009, 7–8). In practice, gender equality turns out to be a broad and complex project. Policies driven by equal opportunities, equal outcomes, or gender mainstreaming do not usually manifest as ideal types, but instead, they are sometimes confused and often conflated. Therefore, some researchers claimed that these frameworks are in fact inseparable. Phillips (1999, 50) argued that "there is no significant space to be inserted between equality of opportunity and equality of outcome when it comes to sexual or racial equality," asserting that "if the outcomes turn out to be statistically related to sex, the opportunities were almost certainly unequal."

Similarly, initiatives undertaken under the banner of gender mainstreaming are often amalgamated with equal opportunities or equal outcomes. Gender mainstreaming may take forms that call for equal access for women to existing structures of opportunity or focus on gender differences in shaping policies and outcomes (e.g., Bacchi and Eveline 2010; True 2010). Even more importantly, what in one setting is considered gender mainstreaming may in a different situation be perceived as equal opportunities or equal outcomes (Lombardo et al. 2009), leading to the conclusion that there is no intrinsic meaning to *gender equality* independent of the context and coexisting political objectives. This prompted Lombardo and colleagues (2009) to suggest that gender equality is an open concept and an inevitably contested policy goal that can be filled with a myriad of meanings that serve various purposes. Policymaking processes lead to the meaning of *gender equality* "being fixed in different concepts," "stretched towards wider meanings or reduced to particular ones," or "bent to fit a variety of other goals" (Lombardo et al. 2009, 3). Such processes of meaning making align the goal of gender equality with preexisting policy environments, institutional structures, and interests of stakeholders. Ultimately, gender equality is shaped by "political goals and intentions" (Lombardo et al. 2009, 7), rather than operating in a sociopolitical and institutional vacuum.

This book approaches gender equality as an unfixed policy goal that is context specific and shaped by political environments in which it operates, and by other competing and coexisting priorities of institutions and stakeholders. While I refrain from defining the goal of gender equality in isolation from the empirical data that will be outlined later in this chapter, my research takes into account the pervasive character of gender inequality and power imbalances across all societal domains that are entrenched in structural discrimination, oppression, and violence, and intersect with other forms of inequality. Just like Squires (2007, 9), in exploring the different approaches to gender equality that will come to the surface in the analysis of the empirics, I find it particularly important to monitor and undertake a critical assessment of "the extent to which they manage to be transformatory while avoiding the pitfalls of assimilation and essentialism" as well as the risk of co-optation.

THE TRAJECTORY OF GENDER EQUALITY

The field of peace and security is considered one of the most masculinist areas of policy and practice (Joachim and Schneiker 2012). The coupling of violent conflict with male-dominated and male-defined security institutions has created a deeply resistant environment to the integration of any gender equality concerns (Ní Aoláin 2016). As a sector, peace and security remained oblivious to gender inequalities that stemmed from the situations of conflict and post-conflict (Cockburn 2012), placing the emphasis on global stability and national interests of powerful states instead. It has taken decades of feminist advocacy to carefully maneuver the goal of gender equality from family affairs to national policy and law, and further to international politics and treaties (Enloe 2014). Only then could gender equality eventually emerge in the sector of global peace and security with the UN Security Council's adoption of the WPS agenda.

Feminist efforts for gender equality and feminist engagements with state and multilateral institutions have a long history. Women's suffrage dates back to the late eighteenth and nineteenth centuries, but even after the hard-won right for (white) women to vote in elections in the twentieth century, gender equality was still considered a private, rather than a public, matter confined to family affairs and relations between women and men in a (heterosexual) family unit. The emergence and spread of the slogan "the personal is political" in the 1960s can be seen as the beginning of the explicit politicizing of gender equality at the state level; through this slogan, feminist advocates underscored that the experience of inequality is intrinsically linked with larger societal structures and infused with power (or lack thereof) (Hanisch 1969).

Greater recognition around the divides between political/personal and public/private led to the proliferation of national policies and laws to support gender equality. Most of these policies targeted the gender equality of women, given the history of enduring oppression and the legacy of feminist movements' advocacy. Scandinavian countries provide a good example of early adoption of gender equality provisions, which were captured by Hernes (1987) under the terms *woman-friendly state* and *state feminism*. For Hernes (1987, 15), these terms referred to "a state where injustice on the basis of gender would be largely eliminated without an increase in other forms of inequality." In this account, the state serves both as a resource and a guardian for gender equality. Yet researchers such as Brown (1995) and Young (2003) claimed that state policies often reproduce power relations and the gendered division of labor between women and men. Specifically, Brown (1995, 170, emphasis in original) pointed to the precarious role of the state in the protection of women from men's domination and violence, suggesting that "such appeals involve seeking protection *from* masculinist institutions *against* men." Later postcolonial scholars further challenged these gender equality policies, most prominent in Scandinavia but also introduced in the United States, the United Kingdom, Australia, and elsewhere around the globe, demonstrating that rather than working toward the universal goal of gender equality, they benefit certain groups of society, typically white, middle-class, educated, abled, and heterosexual women belonging to the ethnic majority. By the same token, such policies marginalize gender inequalities faced by ethnic/racial, socioeconomically disadvantaged, or sexual minorities or women with disabilities, often leaving the preexisting social stratifications fundamentally unchanged (e.g., Yuval-Davis 2006).

The role of the state in forging gender equality remains ambivalent. Nonetheless, there has been a greater recognition of the links between the experience of gender inequality and domestic politics and state institutions. The growing number of legal and policy instruments adopted by states worldwide has over time contributed to greater gender equality opportunities and outcomes across different societal areas (True and Mintrom 2001), most strongly with regards to education and employment (Squires 2007). State aptitudes have become a subject of gender equality indexes that compare performance across the above-mentioned and other areas, including health and political participation, globally (e.g., the World Economic Forum's Global Gender Gap Index, the UN's Human Development Index, the Organisation for Economic Co-operation and Development's Social Institutions and Gender Index, the European Institute for Gender Equality's Gender Equality Index, etc.). Scholars, on their part, have explored gender and welfare regimes to understand the impact of state policies and how they facilitate (or obstruct) the advancement of gender equality, for whom, and under what circumstances (Walby et al. 2012; Krizsan et al. 2014).

The field of international relations has been more resistant to acknowledging the relevance of gender equality (Enloe 2014). International actors, including the UN, have long perceived gender equality in terms of a domestic domain of states, with no place in global politics. Even though a growing body of international relations literature has taken as a task "gendering" global politics (see especially Tickner 1992; 1997; 2010; Tickner and Sjoberg 2013; Ackerly et al. 2006), Tickner and True (2018, 1) aptly pointed out that "international relations came late to feminism." This has only occurred in the last three decades with an increased focus on transnational feminism and the role of multilateral institutions in progressing the goal of gender equality (Kronsell and Svedberg 2011; True 2010). The groundbreaking book *Bananas, Beaches and Bases: Making Feminist Sense of International Politics*, published by Enloe in 1989 and updated in 2014, deserves particular attention because it demonstrated that just like the personal is political, "the personal is also international." That is, the experience of gender inequality is shaped by international processes such as "colonising policies, international trade strategies, and military doctrines" (Enloe 2014, 350). Enloe (2014, 350) further noted that "the international is personal" because the operation of global institutions and foreign policies of states has been contingent on certain gender roles being fulfilled by women as well as on women's emotional labor.

If the field of international relations as a whole has been late to engage with gender equality, then its global peace and security segment came to consider these issues last (Joachim and Schneiker 2012, 530). The traditional separation existed and is still somewhat pervasive in tackling gender inequalities in the contexts of peace/nonconflict on the one hand, and conflict/war on the other, with gender equality concerns being typically underemphasized in the latter (Gierycz 2001; Cockburn 2007). International developments related to gender equality have been undeniable since the mid-twentieth century, but only a fraction of those extended to impact global peace and security. Between the late 1970s and the late 1990s, gender equality emerged as an important issue across the human rights and development pillars of the UN. International instruments—with the primacy of the 1979 Convention on the Elimination of All Forms of Discrimination Against Women and the 1995 Beijing Declaration and Platform for Action—manifest and amplify these developments (Kardam 2004). Gender equality was finally set as a policy goal in the peace and security pillar of the UN with the passing of UNSCR 1325 in 2000 by the Security Council that inaugurated the WPS agenda.

PARADIGMS OF GENDER EQUALITY IN
THE WOMEN, PEACE, AND SECURITY AGENDA

Following decades of advocacy by transnational feminist networks and civil society organizations across the globe, most importantly in conflict-affected countries, the UN Security Council unanimously adopted UNSCR 1325 in 2000 (Cohn et al. 2004; Basu 2016a; 2016b). UNSCR 1325 became the first resolution in the history of the Security Council to address issues of gender equality. Resting on WPS pillars of women's participation, conflict prevention, protection from sexual and gender-based violence, and post-conflict relief/recovery, UNSCR 1325 was welcomed by feminist advocates as a breakthrough in bringing the goal of gender equality to international peace and security. Willett (2010, 142) claimed that the resolution "marked a milestone in the struggle for gender equality in all aspects of peacemaking, peacekeeping and post-conflict recovery." Swaine (2009, 420) maintained that "actions taken under [UN]SCR 1325 should concern themselves with promoting gender equality as an analytical tool for rethinking key policy initiatives, goals, actions, and ideas." Otto and Heathcote (2014, 7) concluded that UNSCR 1325 was "a call for gender equality."

This is not to suggest that UNSCR 1325 was unproblematic for feminist advocates, whether researchers or activists, many of whom pointed to numerous drawbacks of the resolution. The idea of forging gender equality by security institutions and with the use of militaristic means remained among the most contentious, but researchers also criticized UNSCR 1325 for echoing imperialist inclinations of powerful member states of the Security Council and using the façade of gender equality to pursue national security interests (see Ruby 2014; Pratt 2013; Gibbings 2011; Shepherd 2016; Ní Aoláin 2016). Rather, this is to signal that for the great majority of feminist advocates, gender equality was at the heart of UNSCR 1325.

What set UNSCR 1325 apart from any previous resolution adopted by the Security Council—when gender equality is considered—was two intertwined objectives that permeate the WPS pillars. Firstly, UNSCR 1325 called for an increased representation of women in peace and security efforts, including in decision-making bodies. The resolution did not go so far as to explicitly draw on equal opportunities or equal outcomes, or call for the removal of formal barriers to women's equal participation or for the introduction of gender quotas. But given that women were historically excluded from security institutions and women's voices were silenced in peace processes, the call for the expansion of women's roles in conflict prevention, conflict resolution, and post-conflict peacebuilding was nothing less than remarkable.

Secondly and just as importantly, UNSCR 1325 pinpointed the gender-differentiated impact of armed conflict on women, be it gender-based violence, conflict-related trauma and hardship, or other socioeconomic and health burdens carried by women, whether as civilians or combatants, prior to, during, or in the aftermath of conflict. In recognition of this impact, UNSCR 1325 urged for the adoption of a gender perspective, explicitly recalling the term *gender mainstreaming*, in peacekeeping operations and peacebuilding initiatives and programs, and for the protection of women and girls from gender-based violence. Again, the acknowledgment of the gendered impact of conflict as well as issues such as bodily harm and bodily integrity and the gender-differentiated recovery needs of women was a landmark development for the Security Council that had earlier considered these issues irrelevant to the promotion and maintenance of international peace and security (e.g., Anderlini 2011; Jansson and Eduards 2012).

As a matter of clarification, the terms *the WPS agenda* and *UNSCR 1325* are used interchangeably throughout the book unless otherwise specified. I conceive UNSCR 1325 as an umbrella resolution (see also Coomaraswamy 2015) that outlined the overarching vision of the WPS agenda. This vision would be elaborated and operationalized by nine subsequent resolutions (described in detail in chapter 1).

The objectives of UNSCR 1325 highlighting women's *voices* and *experiences* across conflict prevention, conflict resolution, and post-conflict peacebuilding provided the blueprint for my conceptualization of the gender equality goal in operation with the WPS agenda. But how these objectives would be understood in the subsequent resolutions as well as in policies and programs adopted worldwide to implement the WPS agenda would be open to interpretations that serve specific goals, interests, and actors. My empirical analysis brought forth three paradigms of gender equality that emerged within the WPS agenda, focused on security, development, and human rights respectively, resonating with the pillars of the UN system.

Each of the paradigms offers a different approach to gender equality. *The security paradigm of gender equality* focuses on the protection of women and children from conflict-related sexual violence (experience), and advocates for the participation of women in the security sector, most prominently in military and police roles in conflict-affected environments (voice). *The development paradigm of gender equality* underscores the gender-differentiated needs of women in post-conflict recovery (experience), and highlights women's contributions to peace processes and peacebuilding (voice). *The human rights paradigm of gender equality* emphasizes women's decision-making at all levels of peace and security (voice), and calls for the protection of women, and sometimes men too, from all forms of violence, not limited to conflict-related sexual violence, across conflict and peace (experience). While similar at the surface level, these paradigms are distinct in who they target (i.e., what institutions and which women and/or "others"), what they envisage to achieve in the long term and how, and what impact has occurred thus far.

Importantly, the three paradigms of gender equality derive from preexisting structures of the UN and its policy and practice terrains. In line with the UN Charter (Chapter I, art. 1), the UN system traditionally rests on three broad pillars of peace and security, development, and human rights. Gender equality is now recognized as a cross-cutting issue across these typically siloed terrains (see also UNW/2017/6/Rev.1), but this has not always been the case. As previously observed, gender equality had been more established within the human rights and development pillars of the UN system where dedicated efforts predated and shaped the WPS agenda. With the adoption of UNSCR 1325, gender equality finally pervaded the peace and security pillar as well, closing the gap. While broader than the WPS agenda and applicable to the wider context of international politics, the three paradigms of gender equality are in operation with the WPS agenda, producing certain implications for policy and practice.

The coexistence of three distinct paradigms of gender equality within the WPS agenda would create possibilities and limitations for a meaningful change in peace and security. The broad framing of gender equality across the paradigms has facilitated the diffusion of this policy goal across institutions and agendas that were historically most resistant to the incorporation of any gender equality concerns. Many of these stakeholders have been able to tailor and reshape the meaning of gender equality in line with one or more of the paradigms to fit with preexisting policy frames and align with a range of institutional and political interests. In doing so, UNSCR 1325 has undeniably brought new gender awareness and provided a first step for an incremental change in these institutions.

Simultaneously, the WPS agenda's narrow focus on women across the three paradigms, rather than on gender relations and power imbalances in peace and security, has limited the depth and impact of gender equality debates. The emphasis on women has offered an important corrective to the masculinist peace and security policy and practice, which tended to ignore the voices and experiences of women in peace and security. However, this narrow outlook has also diminished the potential of UNSCR 1325 to challenge masculinist structures and processes embedded in peace and security. This is because, for the most part, WPS resolutions, strategies, and action plans address the situation of women in isolation from structural inequalities and systemic discrimination, repeating the key pitfalls of earlier gender equality frameworks. The pursuit of gender equality in peace and security has entailed the commonplace risks of gender equality policymaking identified earlier in this chapter, including assimilation and essentialism as well as co-optation of gender equality for other, sometimes only indirectly related, goals. As time has passed, it has also become evident that the WPS agenda has been pushed in a number of directions, not always retaining an overarching purpose.

GLOBAL, REGIONAL, AND NATIONAL PERSPECTIVES

The tensions between the security, development, and human rights paradigms of gender equality would be pronounced in the implementation of the WPS agenda in the selected case studies. Located at the global, regional, and national level, they include: the UN Security Council (chapter 1), the Association of Southeast Asian Nations and the Pacific Islands Forum (chapter 2), and the governments of the Philippines and Australia (chapters 3 and 4). The goal of gender equality has interplayed in these case studies not only with preexisting gender equality politics and security politics but also with other priorities identified at the intersection of these levels, as well as with the history of colonialism and interactions with the UN. To tease out the complexity of gender equality and the intricacies of power imbalances, the book explores global, regional, and national perspectives on gender equality. This multilevel approach deepens the analysis of gender equality and its ambivalences in operation with the WPS agenda, bringing forth original insights from each of the case studies.

I begin the empirical investigation of gender equality in the WPS agenda with the global level of policymaking, centering the analysis around the politics of the UN Security Council. The WPS agenda has over the years become much more than merely a framework of the Security Council; nonetheless, this bastion of high-level security politics provides the institutional home to it since the passing of UNSCR 1325 in 2000. It is for this reason that the Security Council is the focal point of examination of global processes in chapter 1 that will also depict the three paradigms of gender equality in great detail in relation to WPS resolutions.

In the absence of preexisting notions of gender equality within the Security Council prior to UNSCR 1325 (Basu 2018; Shepherd and True 2014), the WPS agenda and its broad objectives around women's voices and experiences in peace and security had initially generated limited traction. Institutional developments accelerated only from 2008 onward with an increased attention to the heinous impact of conflict-related sexual violence, and by the end of 2015, the three distinct paradigms of gender equality would emerge in operation with the Security Council. While the security paradigm dominated the implementation of the WPS agenda by the Security Council in those years, under the pressure of international civil society, the human rights paradigm has emerged as a strong competitor in more recent years. The growing influence of the human rights paradigm post-2015 has at the same time led to significant resistance from some of the Security Council's members who have opposed the integration of human rights issues with the security-driven agenda of the council. These actors have repeatedly attempted to locate the human rights paradigm of gender equality outside the council's ambit, effectively obstructing institutional developments pertaining to the WPS agenda. Chapter 1 discusses how the coexisting paradigms of gender equality have shaped the operationalization and implementation of the WPS agenda within the Security Council, connecting this to the recent backlash against the agenda.

Chapter 2 moves the interrogation of gender equality in the WPS agenda from the global scenario to that of regional governance. Regional organizations are the major actors that can advocate for the WPS agenda and lead its implementation across a larger number of geopolitically connected states facing similar challenges related to conflict, security, and gender equality (Hudson 2013). The Association of Southeast Asian Nations (ASEAN) and the Pacific Islands Forum (PIF) are two key security organizations in Asia and the Pacific, a region that has over time established some momentum in the implementation of UNSCR 1325 and yet has been generally underexplored in WPS research (Davies and Lee-Koo 2018; Basu 2016a; 2016b; Lee-Koo and Trojanowska 2017).

The regional engagement of Asia and the Pacific with the WPS agenda has been marked, first and foremost, by the resistance toward the security paradigm of gender equality. That is, in their involvement with the WPS agenda, both ASEAN and the PIF have generally rejected securitized notions of gender equality that were prominent at the global level. The security paradigm has been incongruent with regional gender equality politics and simultaneously conceived as a threat to the sovereignty of Asia and the Pacific in the context of the colonial past and present as well as the history of the problematic relationship with the UN. In lieu of the security paradigm, ASEAN and the PIF have opted for the development paradigm and the human rights paradigm respectively in their implementation of the WPS agenda, connecting the agenda to preexisting understandings of gender equality along with regional challenges. Ultimately, the human rights paradigm but especially the development paradigm has resonated with the sociopolitical context in Asia and the Pacific and aligned with priorities set by the region. A juxtaposition of the trajectory of gender equality in the implementation of the WPS agenda by ASEAN and the PIF elucidates the skepticism of Asia and the Pacific toward global discourses that are sometimes perceived as a threat to regional security (see George 2016) rather than a vehicle to improve gender equality in peace and security.

Shifting to the national implementation of the WPS agenda, I explore the traction of gender equality in the Philippines and Australia in chapters 3 and 4. National governments are arguably the most influential actors in the implementation of the WPS agenda (Coomaraswamy 2015). Both the Philippines and Australia have established a strong track record on UNSCR 1325, having introduced WPS policies relatively early in comparison with other countries in the region of Asia and the Pacific, and having gone through the entire lifecycle of WPS implementation. However, the way the Philippines and Australia have approached gender equality in their pursuit of the WPS agenda would be vastly different. That is, the Philippines has adopted the human rights paradigm of gender equality across the policy and practice of the WPS agenda, while Australia's engagement with the agenda has been marked by elements of all three paradigms and has proven largely inconsistent across government departments. Due to their long-standing involvement with UNSCR 1325 and yet contrasting WPS trajectories, I selected the Philippines and Australia as pertinent and revealing case studies from the region of Asia and the Pacific: one that implements the WPS agenda domestically and one that locates WPS implementation in foreign affairs.

In the Philippines, the human rights paradigm of gender equality has driven the engagement with the WPS agenda consistently across the policy and practice. The country has a strong history of national institutionalization of international women's rights frameworks, and the WPS agenda has fitted into the preexisting socio legal context to the point of eventually being integrated into these earlier mechanisms, securing long-term implementation (Veneracion-Rallonza 2013; Trojanowska 2021). The purpose of chapter 3 is to understand the implications and impact of the human rights paradigm of gender equality in this nested case study.

While at the global level, the human rights paradigm was found to be most promising, my empirical analysis of the Philippine case study points to the conclusion that stabilizing the meaning of gender equality in line with human rights principles can have mixed effects. The Philippines' implementation of UNSCR 1325 has produced a significant impact on government departments with preexisting commitments to women's rights that could mitigate the gendered effects of armed conflict without co-opting the goal of gender equality. Simultaneously however, the WPS agenda has had more limited influence on high-level security processes and the upper echelons of the security sector where the human rights paradigm has been incongruent with the dominant militaristic security discourse. As a result, the WPS agenda has not been allowed to address the root causes of state-based violence, especially against minority groups, due to persistent siloes between the policy terrains of human rights and security.

Compared to the Philippines, Australia offers an example of engagement with the WPS agenda driven by a largely incoherent approach to gender equality. Motivated by Australia's international reputation and the bid for the Security Council membership for the 2013–2014 term (Shepherd and True 2014), the Australian government developed an outward-focused WPS policy with elements of all three paradigms of gender equality. This external orientation has made Australia's policy removed from national challenges and at times quite abstract. The high-level discourse on gender equality inclusive of security, development, and human rights issues subsequently failed to translate into a robust implementation strategy (Lee-Koo 2016; Trojanowska 2019). Paradoxically however, in the absence of a streamlined approach to WPS implementation across the government, individual departments had the opportunity to redefine the goal of gender equality in line with their core business and institutional priorities. As chapter 4 explores, this has resulted in significant policy development across the government on the whole, but especially in the security sector, where gender analysis had been historically neglected. At the same time, the implementation has been untargeted and patchy, and the impact on the ground largely unknown, as the Australian government is moving on to the implementation of a second-generation and more focused WPS policy.

In the conclusion, I bring together opportunities, challenges, and risks embedded in the operation of gender equality with the WPS agenda at the juncture of global, regional, and national governance. Being a multifaceted, complex, and cross-cutting issue shaping and shaped by global policymaking processes, regional security politics, and highly politicized environments in conflict-affected countries and in donor countries, gender equality appears to be a process rather than an end goal of the WPS agenda. While it moves fluidly across security, development, and human rights terrains of WPS policy and practice, its meaning has been highly susceptible to the political context in which it has been pursued, whether at the global, regional, or national level.

The process characteristic of gender equality and the fluidity of its purpose has been double-edged. It has without doubt facilitated the far-reaching diffusion of the WPS agenda across a number of actors and political agendas, some of which previously resisted the incorporation of any gender equality concerns. Yet its overall impact has been somewhat constrained and sometimes superficial. In this context, while the meaning attached to gender equality in each of the paradigms has varied and this variation matters greatly in terms of policy and practice implications, the pros and cons of the paradigms for the struggle for gender equality have been less clear-cut. The book ends with a reflection on implications of this research and areas for future research that would benefit both the theory and practice of gender equality in the WPS agenda in the third decade of UNSCR 1325.

EMPIRICALLY DRIVEN RESEARCH

This book is empirically driven. The theorizing of gender equality is a result of careful empirical investigation that combined field research and stakeholder interviews along with policy analysis of documents guiding the implementation of the WPS agenda in different institutional contexts at the global, regional, and national levels. My engagement with the empirical data has been led by a feminist grounded methodology.

The research for this book took me to multiple locations between 2015 and 2017: the UN Headquarters in New York, Manila in the Philippines, and Canberra and Melbourne in Australia. During that time, I had the unequivocal privilege of speaking with nearly seventy policymakers and practitioners in semi-structured interviews, who dedicated their time to a conceptual and practical discussion around working toward greater gender equality in the context of peace and security. The interviewees included representatives from UN agencies, governments, and civil society organizations, and the majority have worked (either at the time of the interview or earlier) with WPS policy and practice, having the ability to shape the implementation of UNSCR 1325 in their respective institutions. Given their high-level status, all interviewees were anonymized to protect their identity. Nonetheless, I will provide non-identifiable details at the start of each empirical chapter to offer the reader an insight into how the interviewees positioned their views on gender equality vis-à-vis their work on the WPS agenda.

The insights of the key stakeholders were juxtaposed with policies governing the implementation of the WPS agenda in dynamic policy and institutional environments, between 2015 and 2021. In each empirical chapter, I will undertake a policy analysis of prime documents that have driven the WPS agenda, whether UN resolutions, regional policies, national plans, or departmental strategies on WPS. Documentary analysis is particularly important because it sets the historical and institutional context that delineates both the opportunities and limitations for meaningful engagement with gender equality. Yet only coupled together with the interviews with WPS stakeholders can the documents tell the actual story behind the meaning and traction of gender equality in WPS policy and practice.

Grounded theory supported my investigation, while "feminist curiosity" guided the inductive process of analysis. The overarching premise of grounded theory is relatively simple: the meaning of analytical concepts, such as the one of gender equality, is not predetermined and forced onto the empirics but instead is anchored in the process of collecting and analyzing data (Ackerly and True 2010; Charmaz 2014). The focal point of this methodology is an inductive process of policy and practice analysis that grounds research findings in the empirics. This process offers a unique opportunity to develop and construct theory immersed in the data (Charmaz 2014). In line with grounded theory, I studied both policy documents and interviews as discourses and accounts that "follow certain conventions and assume embedded meanings" and "tell something of intent and have intended—and perhaps unintended—audiences" (Charmaz 2014, 46–47). Ultimately, my analysis of gender equality rests on the understanding that WPS policies and practices take place within certain geopolitical and institutional settings and serve specific purposes that may or may not be motivated by gender equality. Notwithstanding, they produce implications for how gender equality is conceived and pursued as a goal of the WPS agenda—and toward what ends.

Feminist curiosity is a term coined by Enloe (2004) to describe a form of feminist analysis focusing on power imbalances and women's lives (see also Whooley and Sjoberg 2019). It begins with an open and reflexive mind to question and challenge what has been conventionally seen as "natural." Feminist curiosity allows to explore—and expose—unequal gender power relations, whether in households, in institutions, in societies, or in international affairs (Enloe 2004, 3), demonstrating that they are not inevitable, but rather they are produced and reproduced through a set of norms and institutional practices. In this exploration of unequal gender power relations, feminist curiosity is "taking women's lives seriously" (Enloe 2004, 3). This invokes Enloe's (1989) earlier and crucial investigation into the question of "Where are the women?" in international politics. The critical process of locating women in international politics involves identifying discourses on femininity and complementary discourses on masculinity that drive and feed armed conflicts and peace and security efforts (see Cockburn 2012, 32).

Both power imbalances and women's lives were traditionally ignored in international relations. They continue to be sidelined in global peace and security to this date, despite its focus on power (Tickner and Sjoberg 2013). In this context, I share Whooley and Sjoberg's (2019, 3) conviction that these silences need to be explored "not . . . as absences but instead as indicative of priorities." Similarly, the historical lack of attention to gender equality in peace and security is not simply an omission but rather a manifestation of fundamental global inequality and interests of powerful stakeholders, especially security institutions. However, the growing concern of the peace and security sector with gender equality is also an expression of such interests and has been founded on preexisting structures that have been deeply unequal. The policy goal of gender equality will be studied as such throughout the empirical chapters of the book, starting with the institutional home to the WPS agenda, the UN Security Council.

Chapter 1

The United Nations Security Council

The UN's Women, Peace, and Security (WPS) agenda put forward gender equality as a goal in peace and security. The UN Security Council has provided the institutional home to the agenda since the adoption of Resolution 1325 (UNSCR 1325) in 2000. And yet gender equality was a foreign concept for the Security Council for decades. The history of the Security Council suggests that its member states have been preoccupied with national and global security and demonstrated little interest in gender equality as an issue shaping and shaped by international peace and security efforts prior to 2000. Planting gender equality on this masculinist, "hard security"–driven agenda of the council with the inauguration of the WPS agenda was politically contentious. For many feminist advocates, UNSCR 1325 was groundbreaking (albeit certainly not problem-free) as the first resolution of the Security Council to address gender equality (e.g., Otto and Heathcote 2014; Swaine 2009; Willett 2010). For the Security Council, UNSCR 1325 may have been the proverbial "Trojan Horse" (Anderlini 2007, 196). After all, the modus operandi of the Security Council relies on militaristic approaches to security (whereby security is enacted through military interventions) and neoliberal approaches to peace (whereby peace is promoted through the expansion of capitalist market economies), neither being conducive to the reduction of global gender inequality (Duncanson 2016).

This chapter aims to unravel the meaning and purpose of gender equality in operation with the WPS agenda at the level of the Security Council over the past two decades. My empirical analysis brought forth three dominant paradigms under the overarching vision of UNSCR 1325. These paradigms have emerged within the WPS agenda over the years, resonating with the pillars of the UN system, namely security, development, and human rights. They will provide the analytical framework for the engagement with gender equality in the implementation of the WPS agenda not only by the Security Council but also by regional organizations and national governments discussed in the following chapters. Each paradigm implied a distinct conception of gender equality, pushing the implementation of the WPS agenda in a number of directions within and beyond the Security Council. Some of these ideas have created opportunities for a meaningful change in peace and security. Others, however, have led to multiple risks associated with gender equality policymaking, such as assimilation, essentialism, and especially the co-optation of gender equality for different political goals, most prominently global stability and economic growth of post-conflict nations. While certainly linked to gender equality, these other objectives often reproduce structural inequalities and power imbalances embedded in peace and security. In this chapter, I will ultimately juxtapose unique opportunities that the WPS agenda has created for gender equality in global peace and security with multiple challenges that have emerged or remained in this policy area, including the long-standing resistance toward gender equality among some of the Security Council's members, as well the relatively new backlash against the WPS agenda that became most apparent on the eve of the twentieth anniversary of UNSCR 1325.

The analysis of gender equality in the politics of the Security Council draws from UN policy and institutions associated with the WPS agenda, as well as from field research at the UN Headquarters in New York in 2015 and interviews with nineteen policymakers and practitioners. The interviews were distributed between UN agencies (including the UN Security Council, the UN Department of Peace Operations, the UN Department of Political Affairs, the UN Peacebuilding Commission, the UN Entity for Gender Equality and the Empowerment of Women, the UN Development Programme, and the UN Human Rights Council) and international civil society organizations (including multiple member organizations of the leading transnational network in the subject matter area, the NGO Working Group on Women, Peace, and Security). These actors have played a pivotal role in framing the WPS agenda at the level of global policymaking and ensuring that the Security Council's interest in gender equality is sustained over the long haul. Their views have shaped the policy and practice of the WPS agenda, yielding important consequences for how gender equality has been conceived and pursued in global peace and security. While the interviews were conducted back in 2015 during the UN Security Council High-Level Review of Women, Peace, and Security, they are scrutinized in this chapter in the context of policy development at the level of the Security Council over the last twenty years.

This chapter begins with tracing the process by which gender equality entered the UN's peace and security discourse, culminating in the adoption of UNSCR 1325. I follow by situating the WPS agenda within the mandate and institutional structure of the Security Council. The three paradigms of gender equality are discussed subsequently along with policy and institutional developments that supported the implementation of the WPS agenda but in some cases constrained its remit. Thereafter, I identify trends post-2015 and offer a critical assessment of the potential and impact of the WPS agenda on the struggle for gender equality twenty years after UNSCR 1325 had been passed. To this end, I argue that even though the political climate is not favorable to gender equality at the start of the third decade of UNSCR 1325, active resistance may be a sign that change is actually taking place.

GENDER EQUALITY IN THE UN'S PEACE AND SECURITY DISCOURSE

In the history of the UN, global peace and security and gender equality operated in parallel political realms. The former has remained at the forefront of all UN efforts. The latter was typically marginalized on UN political agendas and disjoined from global peace and security debates and decision-making. The fact that situations of conflict and post-conflict have gender-specific causes, effects, and implications (see Cockburn 2012) was not accounted for in high-level policymaking processes for more than a half-century. The importance of gender equality was randomly raised on different UN fora (for an overview, see Gierycz 2001), yet the "hard security"–driven politics of the Security Council lacked gender analysis of conflict and post-conflict situations altogether (Jansson and Eduards 2012). The intersections between the two fields were noted, usually by transnational women's networks and feminist advocates, but it was not until 2000 that the link between global peace and security and gender equality was formally established with the passing of UNSCR 1325. The early discussions of gender equality in international peace and security that paved the way for UNSCR 1325 will be outlined in the following.

The 1945 UN Charter mandated the Security Council with "primary responsibility for the maintenance of international peace and security" (Chapter V, art. 24). The Security Council has remained the most powerful body of the UN, having at its disposition political, legal, and military means in line with Chapters V, VI, VII, VIII, and XII of the UN Charter. The decision-making of the Security Council rests on five permanent members (i.e., China, France, the Russian Federation, the United Kingdom, and the United States), each having the power to water down any resolution with the use of veto, and ten (previously six) nonpermanent elected members representing geographical regions and serving two-year terms (for more, see Basu 2016a; 2016b). Nonpermanent members do not have the veto prerogative, but passing a resolution requires the affirmative vote of at least nine members of the Security Council (Chapter V, art. 27). The majority of decisions transmitted by Security Council's resolutions are binding and implemented by UN member states as well as UN entities, such as the UN Department of Peace Operations (DPO; earlier known as the UN Department of Peacekeeping Operations or DPKO), the UN Department of Political Affairs (DPA) and others.

Gender equality was also noted in the UN Charter, albeit more implicitly and without a direct reference to peace and security. The UN Charter encouraged "respect for the principle of equal rights and self-determination of peoples" as well as "respect for human rights and for fundamental freedoms for all without distinction to race, sex, language, or religion" (Chapter I, art. 1). That gender equality was regarded of some importance even in the early years of the UN was manifested in the establishment of the UN Commission on the Status of Women (CSW) in 1946 with the guiding principle that "men and women shall have equal rights" (E/281/REV.1, para. 9). However, being a functional commission of the UN Economic and Social Council, the CSW has historically exhibited limited influence on the Security Council and on large political processes of the UN, overall. Outcome documents of the CSW typically take the form of agreed conclusions that are limited to recommendations for UN member states to consider. Ultimately, there is no direct implementation mechanism associated with agreed conclusions, and the power of the CSW is negligible in comparison to the Security Council's.

The 1970s and 1980s saw important institutional developments around gender equality within the UN system, including the establishment of a dedicated agency, the UN Development Fund for Women (UNIFEM), which was later turned into the UN Entity for Gender Equality and the Empowerment of Women (UN Women). However, gender equality in situations of conflict and post-conflict continued to be neglected. The major international bill of women's rights, the 1979 Convention on the Elimination of All Forms of Discrimination Against Women (CEDAW), which called for the removal of any formal barriers for women in line with the idea of equal opportunities and equal treatment before the law, laid out a set of sociopolitical objectives to tackle problems that obstruct gender equality, be it legal discrimination, gender-based violence, or economic disparities. But with the exception of a brief passage in its preamble, CEDAW failed to address gender equality in relation to situations of conflict and post-conflict.

The 1985 Nairobi Forward-Looking Strategies for the Advancement of Women paid slightly more attention to gender equality in conflict, particularly through the broadening of the understanding of peace and security beyond the absence of war. It recognized that "peace is promoted by equality of the sexes, economic equality, and the universal enjoyment of basic human rights and fundamental freedoms" (UNGA 1985). These early mentions of gender equality in conflict and post-conflict settings were relatively vague and typically confined gender to sex, limiting the consideration to women. Furthermore, they were confined to normative documents encouraging action (such as agreed conclusions or outcome documents of the UN World Conferences on Women), as opposed to legal texts authorizing such action (such as resolutions or treaties).

Powerful UN bodies associated with international peace and security were much slower in recognizing the relevance of gender equality. It was only the horrific stories of widespread sexual violence in the mid-1990s, particularly the 1994 Rwandan Genocide and the 1992–1995 Bosnian Genocide, that raised the global awareness of the gender-differentiated impact of armed conflicts and the need to address it as part of broader peace and security efforts (Engle 2005). Feminist advocates built on this growing interest in the heinous impact of conflicts on women during the Fourth World Conference on Women. Adopted during the conference, the 1995 Beijing Declaration and Platform for Action (UNGA 1995)—or BPA for short—established and popularized the strategy of gender mainstreaming to ensure a more systematic integration of a gender perspective in every policy and program. Moreover, the BPA dedicated Platform E to "Women and Armed Conflict." The consideration of gender equality was not confined to conflict-related sexual violence, with Platform E attending to a broader set of objectives, such as equal participation and decision-making in conflict resolution, promotion of the culture of peace, protection of women and girls from human rights violations, and special protection of refugee and displaced women. In doing so, the BPA for the first time addressed issues of gender equality in conflict and post-conflict situations more comprehensively.

Discussions initiated at the Fourth World Conference on Women continued during the 42nd CSW in 1998 and were subsequently incorporated in its agreed conclusions (E/1998/INF/3/Add.2). Yet the 42nd CSW altered the earlier approach to gender equality. According to Cockburn (2007, 140), during the conference, "the emphasis of the activists shifted subtly from getting armed conflict on to the UN's 'woman agenda' to getting 'women and armed conflict' on to the main agenda [of the UN]." In line with the idea of gender mainstreaming, gender equality in conflict and post-conflict contexts was moved from the UN discourse on women and from the primary responsibility of peripheral agencies such as the CSW or UNIFEM and issues of human rights and development toward the terrain of peace and security and the mandate of the UN's "bastion of high politics," the Security Council (Shepherd and True 2014, 258). The process of institutionalizing links between gender equality and global peace and security began shortly after. The 1998 Rome Statute of the International Criminal Court, in force since 2002, was a breakthrough in addressing conflict-related sexual violence, providing that rape and other forms of sexual violence—whether against women or men— may be considered a crime against humanity and a war crime, and charged accordingly (A/CONF.183/9; see also Sivakumaran 2007). International civil society organizations such as Women's International League for Peace and Freedom (WILPF) and the International Alert continued to lobby the Security Council to consider broader issues around women's contributions to international peace and security and women's participation in decision-making related to conflict prevention, conflict resolution, and post-conflict peacebuilding (Anderlini 2011). These organizations advocated tirelessly for the expansion of the narrow focus on sexual violence that dominated gender equality debates back in the 1990s.

The increased pressure from transnational women's networks and the mobilization around gender equality built momentum in the Security Council in 2000 (Tryggestad 2009). In March, the then president of the Security Council, Bangladeshi ambassador Anwarul Chowdhury, released a press statement dedicated to "Women's Rights and International Peace." The statement recognized that "peace is inextricably linked with equality between women and men," affirming that "the equal access and full participation of women in power structures and their full involvement in all efforts for the prevention and resolution of conflicts are essential for the maintenance and promotion of peace and security" (SC/6816).

In May, another nonpermanent member of the Security Council, Namibia, hosted in cooperation with the DPKO a workshop dedicated to "Mainstreaming a Gender Perspective in Multidimensional Peace Support Operations." The Windhoek Declaration and the Namibia Plan of Action adopted during the workshop emphasized that "in order to ensure the effectiveness of peace support operations, the principles of gender equity and equality must permeate the entire mission, at all levels" (S/2000/693). Neither the presidential press statement (SC/6816) nor the Windhoek Declaration and the Namibia Plan of Action (S/2000/693) shied away from the language of gender equality. Hence, they laid conceptual foundations for UNSCR 1325 passed by the Security Council just a few months later, turning a new page in the history of gender equality.

UNSCR 1325 AND THE VISION OF GENDER EQUALITY

On October 31, 2000, the members of the Security Council unanimously adopted UNSCR 1325, the first of resolutions on WPS and the first resolution in the council's history to address gender equality. Resting on the pillars of women's participation, protection from sexual and gender-based violence, conflict prevention, and post-conflict relief/recovery, UNSCR 1325 brought forth two broad objectives strictly relevant to gender equality. These mainly focused on the need for peace and security efforts to account for gender-differentiated impacts of armed conflict and insecurity, and the need for equal participation in peace and security governance. In doing so, the resolution provided a "key" to the Security Council's door (Ruby 2014, 174) and to the consideration of issues of gender equality as part of the UN's peace and security discourse. In order to understand the institutional context of this crucial milestone for the struggle of gender equality in peace and security, the WPS agenda will be situated within the mandate and politics of the Security Council that have provided the ramifications for how gender equality would be tackled in the following years.

UNSCR 1325 inaugurated a new thematic agenda of the Security Council, one dedicated to WPS. The WPS agenda was part of a broader and relatively recent development in the Security Council, namely the consideration of thematic issues and "soft issues" in particular (see Basu 2016a; 2016b; Otto 2010). The business of the Security Council evolves around three major types of problems: general matters related to the Security Council's rules and procedures, country-specific concerns pertaining to a given conflict in a country on the Security Council's agenda, and thematic issues that encompass cross-cutting problems considered critical to the promotion and maintenance of international peace and security. Most of the issues brought to the attention of the council pertain to a specific contemporary armed conflict. Decisions with regards to these conflicts are conveyed through country-specific resolutions, passed under Chapter VII of the UN Charter. This is important to note because Chapter VII has the power to authorize or renew peacekeeping missions, impose sanctions, or establish ad hoc tribunals, among other measures. Provisions stipulated under Chapter VII are legally binding and enforceable. By contrast, thematic and geographically unspecific resolutions, including UNSCR 1325 and nine resolutions on WPS that would follow over the next twenty years, provide a normative compass for the Security Council yet are not formally binding (e.g., Swaine 2017; Barrow 2016). They can establish certain institutional mechanisms, but thematic resolutions are typically adopted under Chapter VI of the UN Charter (or less commonly, under Chapter VIII) and decisions they convey are generally limited to noncoercive measures.[1]

The surge in the Security Council's preoccupation with "soft issues" was most notable from the late 1990s and the early 2000s, with the emergence of three distinct thematic agendas: Children and Armed Conflict, Protection of Civilians, and WPS. It was motivated by the council's interest in expanding its legitimacy over issues that did not traditionally fall under the remit of country-specific resolutions (Otto 2010; Basu 2016a; 2016b). This context defined from the outset the boundary and parameters within which the WPS agenda would operate. Gender equality, by extension, has been conceived as a cross-cutting "soft issue" and placed within the weaker accountability segment of the Security Council.

The positionality of the WPS agenda within the Security Council was not the only challenge to the early struggle for gender equality in peace and security. As a matter of fact, UNSCR 1325 failed to mention *gender equality* explicitly in any of the eighteen operative paragraphs. Operative paragraphs of Security Council's resolutions call for action as opposed to preambulatory clauses that merely express the council's recognition of certain matters. The lack of direct mentions of the term in the body of the resolution has been indicative of the Security Council's resistance to address gender equality under its mandate (see also Simić 2010; Swaine 2017). As the council's vote on any resolution is typically preceded by highly political negotiations between the members and behind closed doors, using language on gender equality would have potentially put UNSCR 1325 at the risk of failure to pass.

Notwithstanding, gender equality permeates UNSCR 1325 (e.g., Otto and Heathcote 2014; Swaine 2009; Willett 2010). The resolution resonated with the preexisting discourses around gender equality in conflict and post-conflict (Gierycz 2001), and at the same time, it brought new elements to the Security Council's discussion of peace and security (Jansson and Eduards 2012). Two of them are particularly significant. Firstly, UNSCR 1325 emphasized the importance of women's participation and leadership in peace and security efforts (e.g., O'Rourke 2014). In the very first four operative paragraphs, the resolution urged the UN, member states, and civil society actors to increase the representation of women in high-level roles traditionally dominated by men: in national, regional, and international decision-making bodies; in field operations (as military observers, civilian police, human rights, and humanitarian personnel); and at the UN Headquarters (as special envoys and special representatives of the secretary-general) (S/RES/1325, OP 1-4). Secondly, UNSCR 1325 acknowledged the gender-differentiated impact of conflict and post-conflict situations. In recognition of this impact, the resolution called on all parties to conflicts to ensure the protection of women and girls from human rights violations, especially from gender-based violence (S/RES/1325, OP 9-11). It urged the integration of a gender perspective into peacekeeping operations and for the delivery of gender-sensitive training to troops prior to deployment (S/RES/1325, OP 5-8). It also encouraged the consideration of the gender-differentiated needs of women in combat, displacement, and humanitarian contexts (S/RES/1325, OP 12-14). Put simply, UNSCR 1325 set on the agenda of the Security Council and elevated issues of women's *voices* in peace and security decision-making and women's *experiences* of armed conflict and insecurity. These issues provided a basis for a broad framing of the gender equality goal. It was entrenched in CEDAW (explicitly mentioned in S/RES/1325, OP 9) with its underlying rule of nondiscrimination on the basis of sex/gender and the guiding principle of equal treatment of women and men, as well as in the BPA (referenced in S/RES/1325, preamble) with its incentive to take into account the gendered impact of any policy or program on women in line with the idea of gender mainstreaming.

UNSCR 1325 did not escape the shortcomings of preexisting discourses on gender equality in peace and security. On the whole, the resolution imagined gender equality as an issue affecting women and girls exclusively, failing to recognize power imbalances in peace and security policy and practice as well as structural issues around violence against women and unequal participation. But the emphasis on women's agency and the range of roles that women play in conflict prevention, conflict resolution, and post-conflict peacebuilding was certainly groundbreaking in the context of the Security Council, as was the acknowledgment of the impact of armed conflicts on women. These elements were capitalized on in the first Report of the Secretary-General on Women, Peace, and Security, published in 2002. The report is important to note because it mapped challenges to the achievement of "the goal of gender equality in relation to peace and security" (S/2002/1154), making gender equality an explicit objective of the WPS agenda for the first time.

That the Security Council was not ready to embrace this broad framing of gender equality became evident in the lack of substantive engagement with the WPS agenda in the early years of UNSCR 1325. The resolution, while certainly a breakthrough in bringing the issues of gender equality to the Security Council's patriarchal decision-making structures, established no institutional mechanism to support the implementation of the WPS agenda. UNSCR 1325 requested the Security Council to remain vigilant to WPS concerns, including through periodic reporting and through consultations with civil society organizations (S/RES/1325, OP 15–18). Beyond this, however, few developments around the WPS agenda could be observed within the Security Council. The System-Wide Action Plan for the Implementation of Security Council Resolution 1325 (presented as part of the 2005 Report of the Secretary-General on Women, Peace, and Security, see S/2005/636), while significant at the level of the UN, might have weakened the Security Council's ownership of the WPS agenda, placing it complacently on the shoulders of agencies with a preexisting commitment to gender equality, including the DPA, the DPO, UN Women, the UNDP, the Office of the UN High Commissioner for Human Rights, and the World Bank. The WPS agenda remained on the Security Council's program of work and continued to be discussed annually, something that cannot be said about all thematic agendas of the Security Council (e.g., one related to HIV/AIDS). Yet the WPS agenda was unfavorably compared to Children and Armed Conflict and

Protection of Civilians agendas (e.g., Swaine 2009, 409–10), both of which were relatively quickly followed by the creation of subsidiary organs and the introduction of other provisions. By contrast, the WPS agenda had to wait nearly another decade for further developments within the Security Council to occur; similar to the struggle for gender equality in peace and security.

THE EMERGENCE OF PARADIGMS
OF GENDER EQUALITY

After the hiatus following the adoption of UNSCR 1325, the developments around the WPS agenda accelerated rapidly starting in mid-2008. The Security Council passed as many as seven subsequent resolutions on WPS just between 2008 and 2015 (i.e., UNSCRs 1820, 1888, 1889, 1960, 2106, 2212, and 2242). The broad vision of UNSCR 1325 that highlighted women's voices and experiences in conflict and post-conflict situations remained at the forefront of the WPS agenda, but these objectives were reinterpreted to meet certain priorities of the Security Council in the light of the changing optics. By 2015, three distinct paradigms of gender equality emerged in the operation with the WPS agenda, resonating with the UN pillars of security, development, and human rights respectively. Each of these paradigms implied a distinct understanding of the goal of gender equality as well as how it ought to be pursued. Yet ideas advocated within the different paradigms did not necessarily align and were contested, whether by the Security Council's members, by other UN agencies, or by international and local civil society organizations. Their impact on the global policymaking has been uneven and ambiguous, as will be discussed in relation to each paradigm and how it has been operationalized within WPS resolutions.

THE SECURITY PARADIGM

State-centric security provides the conventional lens through which the Security Council approaches any given objective placed on its agenda. Gender equality was not immune to this trend, often described as "securitization," that is, a process of framing non-military issues as global or national security matters (e.g., Hudson 2009). In the context of the WPS agenda, it quickly became apparent that protection from sexual violence—and, to a lesser extent, participation in the security sector—connected better with the Security Council's mandate and identity than the broad claims of UNSCR 1325. These issues provided the basis for *the security paradigm of gender equality*, which unveiled experiences of conflict-related sexual violence against women (and children) and emphasized the role of women in the police and military, especially in efforts to respond to such violence. This narrow understanding of gender equality has had significant influence on the Security Council as well as other security actors, but it has also entailed some of the key risks of gender equality policymaking, especially co-optation of the goal of gender equality for other objectives, and assimilation of women in the security sector. For this reason, it has received mixed reviews from the outside of the Security Council, especially from international civil society organizations.

Protection of Women (and Children) from Conflict-Related Sexual Violence

The Security Council's first open debate on sexual violence in conflict can be seen as the inception of the security paradigm of gender equality. Convened in 2008, the debate resulted in the unanimous adoption of UNSCR 1820, the second resolution on WPS, which acknowledged the calamitous impact of conflict-related sexual violence. In the opening operational paragraph, the resolution emphasized that

> Sexual violence, when used or commissioned as a tactic of war in order to deliberately target civilians or as a part of a widespread or systematic attack against civilian populations, can significantly exacerbate situations of armed conflict and may impede the restoration of international peace and security. (S/RES/1820, OP 1)

The systematic character of sexual violence in armed conflict was noted earlier in the 1998 Rome Statute of the International Criminal Court. But it was not until the passage of UNSCR 1820 that the slogan "rape is a weapon of war" became more commonly used within the chamber of the Security Council. UNSCR 1820 called for "equal protection under the law" and "equal access to justice" for victims of conflict-related sexual violence (S/RES/1820, OP 4). In all of this, the resolution framed gender equality as an issue of protection, and the effort to contain widespread sexual violence in situations of conflict as a means to national and global stability.

The focus on protection from conflict-related sexual violence revitalized the WPS agenda that had seen limited traction up to that point. It confidently placed the WPS agenda back into the deliberation of the Security Council, driving significant institutional developments in the following years. Protection became the theme of subsequent resolutions on WPS passed between 2009 and 2013 (i.e., UNSCRs 1888, 1960, and 2106). These resolutions created concrete protection mechanisms at multiple levels. At the level of UN governance, UNSCR 1888 established the Office of the Special Representative of the Secretary-General on Sexual Violence in Conflict to support high-level decision-making of the UN in tackling this problem (S/RES/1888, OP 4). At the level of UN operations, UNSCR 1888 urged for the deployment of Teams of Experts on Sexual Violence in Conflict and the identification of Women Protection Advisors (S/RES/1888, OP 8 and 12), while UNSCR 1960 requested strengthening reporting and documentation of sexual violence through the Monitoring, Analysis, and Reporting Arrangements (S/RES/1960, OP 8). At the level of conflict-affected countries, UNSCR 2106 called for the adoption of targeted sanctions against perpetrators of sexual violence in situations of conflict (S/RES/2106, OP 13). By the end of 2013, the Security Council put in place a relatively strong normative framework on protection of women (and children) from conflict-related sexual violence (Coomaraswamy 2015; Huvé 2018).

The institutional developments around protection were significant, but they implied the narrowest understanding of gender equality within the WPS agenda. Issues of gender equality were confined to protection (as opposed to taking into account other elements of the WPS agenda such as participation), to women (and children) (as opposed to considering the role of men and gender power relations in acts of sexual violence), and to conflict-related sexual violence (as opposed to acknowledging other forms of gender-based violence as well as the continuum between structural and physical violence).

First of all, the remit of the organs and provisions established by UNSCRs 1820, 1888, 1960, and 2106 was circumscribed to protection. For example, the Office of the Special Representative of the Secretary-General on Sexual Violence in Conflict is mandated to tackle the protection aspect of the WPS agenda exclusively. This contrasted with the Office of the Special Representative of the Secretary-General for Children and Armed Conflict that adopted a more holistic approach to the implementation of the Children and Armed Conflict agenda.

Secondly, the resolutions fell into the trap of victimization, whereby women (and children) are conceived to be merely victims in need of (masculinist) protection (see also Young 2003). Not only did this undermine women's agency, but it also diminished the impact of sexual violence on men, excluding them from the very concept of gender equality. With the exception of a single reference in the preamble to UNSCR 2106, the resolutions neglected men's victimhood in spite of it being an increasingly recognized concern in conflict and post-conflict situations (e.g., Sivakumaran 2007; Zarkov 2007; Lewis 2014). In doing so, the resolutions further ignored gender power relations that drive sexual violence and make it so effective as a weapon of war.

Thirdly and relatedly, the focus on protection from conflict-related sexual violence diverted the attention from other forms of violence, including structural violence, that are exacerbated in the situations of conflict and enable wartime sexual crimes. Coomaraswamy (2015, 71) similarly found that the protection framework laid out by the Security Council was "less effective in addressing the cause: in other words, in challenging the gender norms that trigger violence before, during, and after war" (see also Davies and True 2015). The early appraisal of the security paradigm of gender equality with its strong orientation toward protection was ultimately ambivalent for the political struggle for gender equality. It certainly created much-needed momentum for the WPS agenda within the Security Council. But it has taken the attention of the Security Council away from more progressive elements of the agenda, such as participation of women in peace and security efforts.

Inclusion of Women in the Security Sector

While preoccupied with protection, some of the Security Council's resolutions on conflict-related sexual violence integrated issues of participation, in response to international civil society's advocacy for broadening the narrow outlook. This development expanded slightly the notion of gender equality within the security paradigm, but the focus remained rather constrained. The call for women's participation was scattered across these resolutions and typically limited to preambulatory clauses with no associated implementation measures. It was also predominantly targeted at the security sector and thereby linked to the effectiveness of police and military forces in tackling conflict-related sexual violence. The resolutions connected the presence of female peacekeepers to improved reporting of sexual violence by local populations (S/RES/1960, preamble) and building a more responsive security sector at national levels (S/RES/1888, preamble). Once more, gender equality was perceived as a tool to security-driven ends.

The Security Council did not put in place any bureaucratic mechanism or strategy (such as gender quotas or targets) in support of women's inclusion in the security sector, whether in UN peacekeeping operations or in member states' security forces. Nonetheless, the WPS resolutions have contributed to a debate around removing formal barriers for women to serve in the military and police roles in challenging conflict-affected environments, especially in combat (e.g., Trisko Darden 2015; Egnell 2016). International civil society has been divided with respect to this development. Some saw in it a distinct opportunity for a long-term and transformative change for greater gender equality from within the security sector, as apparent in the following interview excerpt:

> To answer your question, "What does gender equality mean in this context?" it also
> means having a higher percentage of women in the security sector, in the police and

the military. We believe that by increasing the number or percentage of women in
the security sector, there will be a greater possibility of making the framework of
security broader and more comprehensive. (International CSO 1, interview)

The interviewee elaborated on the belief that with greater inclusion of women
in the security sector, the dominant peace and security discourse would
expand onto nontraditional security issues, such as economic, health, or
personal security, that are more directly linked to gender equality outcomes.
However, such voices belonged to a minority of international civil society
actors I interviewed in New York, and the act of connecting the increased
number of women in certain roles to changes with regards to organizational
cultures and political agendas has been debated in scholarly literature on gender equality (e.g., Squires 2007; Krook 2006; Celis et al. 2008). The call for
the inclusion of women in police and military roles resonated most strongly
with the risk of assimilation, that is, a process that integrates women into
existing (masculinist) structures without altering these structures (see also
Squires 2007).

Other interviewees similarly claimed that the incentive to include women
in the police and military roles is a dangerous one, both to women and to
the endeavor for gender equality. They pointed out that without challenging
the current structures and identity of the security sector, the enlistment of
women puts them at a high risk of sexual abuse and harassment, not only
by counterpart security forces but also by male colleagues in their own
ranks (see also True and Parisi 2013). Furthermore, feminist researchers and
activists emphasized that women's participation in the security sector and
especially in the military is an extension of militarism and militarization that
contribute to institutions of power that drive armed violence and produce
gender inequalities in the first place (Enloe 2000; Duncanson and Woodward
2016). Ruby (2014, 174), formerly the director of Women's International
League for Peace and Freedom (WILPF) UN Office, explicitly stated that
"militarism and armed conflict are completely at odds with the goals of gender equality." For these feminist advocates, the inclusion of women in the
military sabotages gender equality both in the short and long term (see also
Cohn et al. 2004).

In sum, the security paradigm of gender equality quickly gained the support
of the Security Council and dominated the peace and security discourse on
gender equality. But outside the Security Council's chamber, many accused
it of disingenuous interest in supporting the goals of gender equality as part
of the WPS agenda. The resolutions on conflict-related sexual violence
refrained from referring to gender equality explicitly in operative paragraphs
(with the exception of S/RES/2106, OP 20). While these resolutions recognized the heinous impact of sexual violence, they did not emphasize issues

of bodily integrity and bodily harm but rather positioned sexual violence as a security matter with relevance to national and global stability. Women's inclusion in the security sector was similarly a tool to improve operational effectiveness rather than an issue of equal labor rights (cf. MacKenzie 2012). In this context, securitization of gender equality can be seen as a form of co-optation, whereby gender equality is set to fulfil security-driven objectives of the Security Council. Associated with it was the risk of assimilation, a process that integrates women into the security sector without challenging its masculinist structures. Framing gender equality as a global and national security matter and conceiving women as a means toward that end certainly elevated the issues of gender equality on the agenda of the Security Council. Simultaneously, these processes constricted the remit of the WPS agenda, failed to address the root causes of structural inequalities and violence, and reinforced militaristic responses to conflict without addressing problematic organizational cultures within the security sector. In the face of the growing criticism from international civil society organizations, especially trans-national women's networks, the Security Council adopted resolutions that shifted the focus toward the terrains of development and human rights, where the effort for gender equality had been more established.

THE DEVELOPMENT PARADIGM

A development lens played an important role in shaping how many, particularly UN agencies with preexisting gender equality commitments and some of international and local civil society organizations, think of gender equality in the context of the WPS agenda. These actors pointed out to the nexus between the issues of development and security, and the role of women in advancing both areas. However, the Security Council's ownership of the WPS agenda discouraged the integration of developmental issues due to persistent siloes between security and development policy and practice within the UN, the latter typically addressed outside the Security Council by agencies such as the United Nations Development Programme (UNDP) and UN Women.

Consequently, *the development paradigm of gender equality* would be the least prominent in operation with the WPS agenda at the level of the Security Council, with only one resolution dedicated to it in full (i.e., UNSCR 1889). Nevertheless, it has brought new elements to the Security Council's conception of gender equality, in particular around women's empowerment and participation in peace processes and peacebuilding, and women's needs in post-conflict recovery. While this has broadened the limited discussion of gender equality, the development paradigm has entailed another major risk of gender equality policymaking, namely essentialism.

Empowerment of Women in Peace Processes and Peacebuilding

It is important to start by recognizing that UNSCR 1889 would become the first resolution to explicitly mention *gender equality* in an operative paragraph. The resolution called for the promotion of gender equality within UN missions and the mobilization of resources for the advancement of gender equality as part of post-conflict peacebuilding (S/RES/1889, OP 7 and 14). With the emphasis on socioeconomic and developmental challenges in post-conflict situations, UNSCR 1889 sat somewhat oddly within the Security Council that is typically concerned with active armed conflicts. Adopted in 2009, only a week after the passing of UNSCR 1888 that was dedicated to conflict-related sexual violence, it was almost certainly impelled by international civil society's criticism of the Security Council's preoccupation with protection. UNSCR 1889 addressed this criticism in the preamble, "stressing the need to focus not only on protection of women but also on their empowerment in peacebuilding" (S/RES/1889, preamble).

Women's empowerment is indeed at the forefront of UNSCR 1889. The resolution called for improved participation during all stages of peace processes, in peacebuilding, in aid management and planning, and in UN missions (S/RES/1889, OP 1, 15, and 4). By the same token, UNSCR 1889 expanded the limited scope of the security paradigm of gender equality where participation was confined to the security sector and to roles in which women's presence was a means to support efforts to combat conflict-related sexual violence. Moreover, UNSCR 1889 dived into socioeconomic and structural inequalities that hinder women's participation in peace and security. It noted with concern:

> The persistent obstacles to women's full involvement in the prevention and resolution of conflicts and participation in post-conflict public life, as a result of violence and intimidation, lack of security and lack of rule of law, cultural discrimination and stigmatization, including the rise of extremist or fanatical views on women, and socioeconomic factors including the lack of access to education. (S/RES/1889, preamble)

Ultimately, UNSCR 1889 acknowledged some of the deep causes of gender inequality and discrimination of women in post-conflict societies, including political, legal, and socioeconomic barriers to participation. But while the call for women's participation in peace processes and peacebuilding would be welcomed by some civil society organizations, especially in conflict-affected countries, it would be followed by the gender stereotyping of the role played by women in these processes. UNSCR 1889 challenged negative attitudes around women's decision-making capability and reoriented the Security Council toward the issue of participation (UNSCR 1889, OP 1 and preamble); however, the resolution replaced these negative beliefs with a set of different assumptions that had more positive connotations but continued to be gender stereotyping. In line with UN Women's long-standing argument that "women's participation strengthens peacebuilding via improved family welfare, community security, and decision-making that is more responsive to a diverse set of needs" (Douglas 2015, 90; see also Castillo Diaz and Tordjman 2012), UNSCR 1889 portrayed women's empowerment as a means to ensure the well-being of families and communities. For example, the resolution stressed "the key role women can play in reestablishing the fabric of recovering society" (S/RES/1889, preamble). An interviewee from the UNDP similarly emphasized that "to bring women to peace process is also to bring the development nexus" (UNDP, interview). In providing an additional leverage to advocate for women's empowerment in post-conflict peacebuilding, such framing of gender equality has also reinforced the sociopolitical constructs of gender roles as well as the gendered division of labor, whereby women are expected to fulfil certain—typically caretaking—responsibilities in society.

Gender-Differentiated Needs of Women in Post-Conflict Recovery

The second of aspect of the development paradigm of gender equality articulated in UNSCR 1889 was the strong emphasis on the gender-differentiated needs of women in post-conflict situations. It is generally uncommon for the Security Council to pay attention to the needs of conflict-affected populations beyond physical security and protection of civilians from conflict-related violence. And yet UNSCR 1889 encouraged UN member states and civil society to support "better socioeconomic conditions" through education, employment, and access to health and other services (S/RES/1889, OP 10 and preamble). Mentions of sexual and reproductive health are perhaps most significant because they touched on—even though only indirectly—an issue fundamental to gender equality: bodily autonomy. An astonished interviewee from an international civil society organization commented on this issue by saying: "Who would ever think that the Security Council would be talking about the issues of sexual and reproductive healthcare? That was nowhere in anyone's imagination before" (International CSO 1, interview). Once again, UNSCR 1889 broadened the narrow security paradigm to include a more encompassing set of social, economic, political, legal, and health issues that impact gender equality opportunities and outcomes.

While bringing all these new elements to the Security Council's discourse on gender equality in peace and security was significant, UNSCR 1889 did little to address them through concrete action. Institutionally, the traction of the development paradigm within the Security Council was very limited. UNSCR 1889 requested a progress report to analyze specific needs of women and girls in post-conflict situations and challenges to women's participation in peacebuilding (S/RES/1889, OP 19). Beyond this, the effort to operationalize the development paradigm was rather minimal. The Report of the Secretary-General on Women's Participation in Peacebuilding (A/65/354–S/2010/466), released in 2010 and tabled in the Security Council and the UN General Assembly, outlined a brief Seven-Point Action Plan on Gender Responsive Peacebuilding that put forward a series of recommendations. Most significantly, it urged each UN entity to dedicate at least 15 percent of UN peacebuilding funds to projects that respond to women's needs, advance gender equality, or empower women. But the call on UN agencies remained just this: a recommendation with no associated accountability mechanism.

The primary focus on women's empowerment coupled with the relatively comprehensive approach to gender-differentiated needs of women recovering from conflict provided a new perspective on gender equality in the context of the WPS agenda. Yet in broadening the understanding of gender equality in peace and security to include socioeconomic issues, the development paradigm did not renounce gender norms that underlie societal inequalities but only altered them. As a result of attributing certain qualities to women, UNSCR 1889 contributed to essentializing their roles and the gender difference. For this very reason, the development paradigm was dismissed by some of my interviewees who emphasized that a "straight participation approach that brings in women only in a sort of gender-stereotyped role . . . is not about gender equality" (International CSO 9, interview; see also Valenius 2007). For many feminist advocates, only an approach driven by human rights would be a genuine path to gender equality in peace and security.

THE HUMAN RIGHTS PARADIGM

While UNSCR 1889 included some progressive albeit problematic ideas of gender equality, the real winds of change came with UNSCR 2122 and mandated by it the UN Security Council High-Level Review of Women, Peace, and Security. Both linked the WPS agenda back to the human rights tradition, echoing the original intent of UNSCR 1325. The *Global Study on the Implementation of United Nations Security Council Resolution 1325*, commissioned as part of the high-level review, explicitly stated that "women's leadership and the protection of women's rights should be always at the forefront—and never an afterthought—in promoting an international peace and security" (Coomaraswamy 2015, 4). Gender quality was ultimately conceived as an issue of full and equal participation in all political processes, especially at the highest levels, and protection from human rights abuses and violations, not limited to conflict-related sexual violence. *The human rights paradigm of gender equality* has been welcomed by international civil society organizations as well as by other feminist advocates from within the UN, many of whom regarded it as the most promising approach, but it has been resisted by some of the Security Council's members. This resistance did not halt the progression in the lead-up to the high-level review that would be a culminating point for gender equality advocacy in peace and security.

Participation of Women in All Political Processes and Decision-Making

Starting with 2013 through to 2015, gender equality gained significant traction in the WPS agenda within the Security Council. UNSCR 2122, passed in 2013, did not refrain from equality language, whether in the preamble or in the body of the resolution. On the contrary, the resolution emphasized that "women's and girls' empowerment and gender equality are critical to efforts to maintain international peace and security" and a crucial part of an integrated approach to sustainable peace (S/RES/2122, preamble and OP 4). Feminist researchers and activists quickly acclaimed UNSCR 2122 "radically different" from previous resolutions (Shepherd 2014, 2). UNSCR 2242, adopted during the 2015 Open Debate on WPS that served as the Security Council High-Level Review of Women, Peace, and Security, continued this trend, "welcoming the emphasis placed on achieving gender equality" (S/RES/2242, preamble). Both UNSCRs 2122 and 2242 explicitly turned to the human rights tradition, noting that "persisting barriers to the full implementation of Resolution 1325 (2000) will only be dismantled through dedicated commitment to women's participation and human rights" (S/RES/2242, preamble; see also S/RES/2122, preamble).

Women's participation was undeniably placed at the center stage once more—this time, however, in the context of all decision-making processes. UNSCRs 2122 and 2242 extended the goal of participation from the police and military roles (as in the security paradigm) as well as from peacebuilding (as in the development paradigm) to all relevant processes, especially formal processes, inter alia in elections and political processes, disarmament, demobilization and reintegration programs, security sector and judicial reforms, and wider post-conflict reconstruction processes (see especially S/RES/2122, OP 4). Furthermore, the resolutions shifted the Security Council's attention toward leadership roles and positions of power and influence where women are typically most marginalized. UNSCR 2242 called for "increased representation of women at all decision-making levels in national, regional and international institutions" and for "women's meaningful inclusion in negotiating parties' delegations to peace talks" (S/RES/2242, OP 1). The resolution also advocated for the appointment of women in UN leadership positions (S/RES/2242, OP 8). UNSCRs 2122 and 2242 emphasized that the successful implementation of the WPS agenda is reliant on women's participation and leadership, but as opposed to the security and development paradigms of gender equality where participation was a means to other ends, these resolutions conceived it as a fundamental right of women.

Protection of Women's Rights in Conflict, Post-conflict, and Nonconflict

A second but equally important aspect of the human rights paradigm of gender equality promoted by UNSCRs 2122 and 2242 was the respect for women's rights and protection from the full range of violations and abuses, noting emerging security challenges. This extended the narrow focus on protection from conflict-related sexual violence to all forms of violence. UNSCR 2242 recognized the unique impact of terrorism and violent extremism on women, expressing the concern about women's rights being deliberately targeted by extremist groups (S/RES/2242, preamble and OP 13–15). The resolution further noted the issue of sexual exploitation and abuse of local populations (S/RES/2242, OP 9–10), bringing to light shameful allegations against UN personnel that had been generally separated from WPS resolutions (Westendorf and Searle 2017). While noting "the changing global context of peace and security," UNSCR 2242 pointed to the global nature of health pandemics long before COVID-19, as it did to the impacts of climate change (S/RES/2242, preamble). In all of this, the human rights paradigm of gender equality conceptualized both violence and participation as occurring on a continuum: across physical and structural violence and across informal and formal decision-making respectively (see Koens and Gunawardana 2020).

The renewed attention to women's leadership and rights was not limited to rhetorical statements. The human rights paradigm of gender equality established some institutional mechanisms at the level of the Security Council and UN operations, three of which are particularly significant. Firstly, the Informal Expert Group on Women, Peace, and Security was set up pursuant to UNSCR 2242 (see S/RES/2242 OP 5) to improve the oversight of the progress made in the implementation of the WPS agenda, including through interactions between the Security Council's members and civil society organizations (see S/2016/1106). As opposed to the Office of the Special

Representative of the Secretary-General on Sexual Violence in Conflict, which focuses exclusively on conflict-related sexual violence, the mandate of the informal expert group encompasses the entire WPS agenda and addresses impediments to its implementation on the whole.

Secondly, the Global Acceleration Instrument for Women, Peace, and Security and Humanitarian Action, later renamed to the Women's Peace and Humanitarian Fund, was created to collect funds to support civil society organizations in implementing the WPS agenda in countries affected by armed conflict. In operation since 2016, it has managed a budget of over $46M, subsidized by donor countries and private sector (UNDP 2021). Both the UN Women's Peace and Humanitarian Fund and the Informal Expert Group on Women, Peace, and Security support the goal of gender equality by allowing civil society—and especially women's organizations—to shape projects and programs in conflict-affected countries and inform decisions of the Security Council.

The third mechanism—Gender Advisors—was more direct. The role of Gender Advisors is similar to Women Protection Advisors, but it links explicitly to "the promotion of gender equality and the empowerment of women in conflict and post-conflict situations" (S/RES/2122, OP 4; see also S/RES/2242, OP 7), once again broadening the earlier focus on conflict-related sexual violence. The appointment of gender advisors was mandated by earlier resolutions (e.g., S/RES/1889, OP 7; S/RES/1960, OP 10; S/RES/2106, OP 8), but with UNSCRs 2122 and 2242 there was both a greater recognition of the important function of this role as well as a shift toward it becoming more senior and more centrally located within the UN system and UN missions, in line with the idea of gender mainstreaming. All three mechanisms ultimately expanded and augmented the remit of the WPS agenda and in doing so enhanced gender equality more comprehensively as a policy goal.

It further deserves to be noted that outside the Security Council, the WPS agenda was also addressed within the human rights pillar of the UN system. Specifically, in October 2013 the CEDAW Committee adopted General Recommendation no. 30 (GR 30) on Women in Conflict Prevention, Conflict, and Post-Conflict Situations, which clarified state and non-state actors' obligations related to CEDAW in conflict, post-conflict, and the state of emergency (CEDAW/C/GC/30; see also Swaine and O'Rourke 2015). In doing so, GR 30 established clear links between UNSCR 1325 and CEDAW and opened for reporting on the progress in implementing the WPS agenda through human rights mechanisms such as the Universal Periodic Review.

For many feminist advocates, the human rights paradigm of gender equality advocated with the WPS agenda offers a real opportunity for sustained, structural, and transformative changes to the gender inequalities and power imbalances embedded in conventional peace and security efforts. An interviewed gender equality expert with background from UN and civil society emphasized that:

> Gender equality is the longer-term, structural change whereby the goal is not just to add women to the table; the goal is to have a conversation about the right of women to be part of decision-making. And the reason they are not there is structural inequalities that tell us to think that it's okay that they are not there. So, for me gender equality is about the transformational, structural changes that need to happen in our societies. (UN/International CSO, interview)

Neither UNSCR 2122 nor 2242 went this far. Nonetheless, in highlighting the centrality of gender equality as a goal of the WPS agenda in its own right, deepening the gender analysis of conflict and post-conflict, in particular around the continuums of violence and participation, and putting in place institutional mechanism to support the implementation of these objectives in collaboration with civil society organizations, the resolutions contributed to an enabling environment for a structural and institutional change. The human rights paradigm ultimately offered an uncompromising and incremental approach that challenges the status quo embedded in gender inequalities and discrimination against women and imagines power and security institutions in a different way. For many of my interviewees, it is the most promising paradigm of gender equality in the operation of the Security Council.

The year 2015 and the high-level review was the high point for the WPS agenda and for gender equality advocacy in peace and security. Gender equality was at the forefront of the Open Debate in October, which that saw an unprecedented number of 113 statements (S/PV.7533). Then–Secretary-General Ban Ki-moon reiterated that "fifteen years ago, resolution 1325 (2000) underscored the pivotal link between gender equality and international peace and security" (S/PV.7533). Members of the Security Council called the high-level review "a new start for more equality" (France) and the year 2015 "crucial for women's rights, the efforts of the United Nations toward gender equality, and strengthening the Women and Peace and Security agenda" (Angola) (see S/PV.7533).

Russia was the only member of the Security Council at that time to explicitly oppose the goal of gender equality. Russian delegation to the UN stated that "gender equality and the advancement of women . . . should be carried out based on the appropriate mandates" (S/PV.7533) and located it once again outside the Security Council's ambit (see also Swaine 2017). Yet neither Russia nor China (known to be less supportive of the WPS agenda; see also Basu 2016a; 2016b) voted against or even merely abstained when UNSCR 2242 was passed, despite the substantive references to gender equality throughout the text of the resolution.

In 2015, voices contesting gender equality appeared both obscured and less influential in shaping the policy and practice of the WPS agenda. One of my interviewees commented on this shift by saying on the very day of the high-level review that "we are moving in the right direction [because] today there is a consensus that we have to look at women and peace from a human rights lens" (UNHRC, interview). But any progress on gender equality is typically volatile, which became evident also in the case of the WPS agenda post-2015.

POST-2015 RESISTANCE TO GENDER EQUALITY

Following the 2015 high-level review, the progression of the WPS agenda initially confirmed a subtle shift in the Security Council's mentality toward greater appreciation of gender equality as a goal in peace and security. There was a general agreement both by the Security Council's members and international civil society organizations that another resolution on WPS was not required at that time, as the existing resolutions provided a relatively comprehensive normative framework that needed to be translated into routine implementation practice. Nonetheless, the council's members continued to advocate for the WPS agenda and gender equality as part of it during annual debates. Notable was, for instance, the title of a debate dedicated to sexual violence in conflict held by the Security Council in April 2018, "Preventing Sexual Violence in Conflict through Empowerment, Gender Equality, and Access to Justice." Taking into account the fact that the Security Council's debates on conflict-related sexual violence were typically limited to addressing such violence in isolation from wider gender inequalities, this was by all means a powerful title. It signaled the Security Council's recognition of sexual violence as linked to broader societal norms as opposed to occurring in a vacuum. It also signaled that issues of gender equality seemingly pierced the peace and security discourse. This rhetoric by itself is not enough to attain the goal of gender equality, but it was a step in that direction.

With increased gender awareness came stronger resistance toward gender equality and progress made over the years. Three distinct trends can be identified in the period post-2015, all of them reducing the impact of the human rights paradigm of gender equality on the actual implementation of the WPS agenda. These were: the co-optation of the WPS agenda for efforts relating to Countering Violent Extremism, the marginalization of women's leadership at the highest levels of the UN, and explicit resistance toward the human rights paradigm of gender equality and backlash on the WPS agenda on the eve of the twentieth anniversary of UNSCR 1325.

The first trend had already started in 2015 following the passing of UNSCR 2242 at the UN Security Council High-Level Review of Women, Peace, and

Security. As briefly noted in the above, UNSCR 2242 linked the WPS agenda to a different agenda of the UN—Countering Violent Extremism—creating a new set of old challenges to the goal of gender equality, especially co-optation of gender equality for security-driven aims. To be sure, the interconnections between women's rights and violent extremism are important and should be addressed by the Security Council in a comprehensive manner. However, the way this has been done in the years following the passing of UNSCR 2242 undermined the focus on women's rights against the intent of the resolution.

In recognition of the growing global threat posed by radicalization, violent extremism, and terrorism, UNSCR 2242 paid attention to the gender-differentiated impact of these acts on the rights of women. The topic of violent extremism was limited to three (out of eighteen) operational paragraphs of UNSCR 2242 (S/RES/2242, OP 11-13) and formulated in a human-rights-based language around gender equality that posited "women's participation, leadership, and empowerment as core to the United Nation's strategy and responses [to violent extremism]" (S/RES/2242, OP 11 and 13). In post-2015 however, these three operative paragraphs have overshadowed the remaining fifteen in ways detrimental to gender equality.

The issue of violent extremism has become the emblem of UNSCR 2242, especially for the security sectors where women and women's rights have been subsequently envisaged as a device for countering violent extremism strategies and planning, and sometimes as a source of intelligence. This, in some cases, put women's lives on the line. The co-optation of the WPS agenda by the Countering Violent Extremism agenda has led to new forms of securitization of gender equality. The pitfalls and real political dangers of linking the WPS agenda to the Countering Violent Extremism agenda have been criticized widely in scholarly literature (e.g., Phelan 2020; Ní Aoláin 2016; Kirby and Shepherd 2016) and were therefore only briefly described in this chapter. Nonetheless, this trend points out to the ease with which the goal of gender equality, even in the most promising paradigm, can be instrumentalized and sacrificed for objectives not directly related to the political struggle for gender equality.

Secondly, but perhaps most importantly, the Security Council has continued to marginalize women's leadership, despite the strong focus on this issue within the human rights paradigm of gender equality and at the high-level review. The 2016 selection of the UN secretary-general, the highest-level role within the UN system, provided a real testing ground for the influence of the WPS agenda on women's participation in positions of power. Since the establishment of the UN in 1945, a woman has never been appointed the UN secretary-general. The Security Council plays the key role in the selection of the secretary-general, who is appointed by the General Assembly on the recommendation of the Security Council (UN Charter 1945, Chapter XV, art. 97). The preferred candidate is determined through a series of straw polls cast by the Security Council's members in a secret ballot. The gender-balanced number of candidates (i.e., seven women and six men) considered for the secretary-general in 2016 was historic. Yet in the lead-up to the Security Council's recommendation, gender bias and male favoritism quickly became apparent, eventually resulting in the selection of a male candidate, António Guterres, over a number of highly qualified and accomplished female candidates. Among them were the former prime minister of New Zealand and the then-head of the UNDP, Helen Clark, and the former deputy minister of foreign affairs of Bulgaria and the then-head of the United Nations Educational, Scientific and Cultural Organization (UNESCO), Irina Bokova.

Guterres has proven to support the goal of gender equality. The Gender Parity Strategy, launched soon after Guterres commenced the office of the secretary-general in 2017, has brought much-needed progress to the involvement of women in the leadership of the UN, a number of them being subsequently appointed as the secretary-general's special representatives and envoys (for details, see S/2018/900). Under Guterres's leadership, the UN described gender-based violence during the COVID-19 pandemic as "the shadow pandemic," further recognizing its impact on women's participation in public life (see UN Women n.d.). On the twentieth anniversary of UNSCR 1325, Guterres highlighted that women's leadership is "essential to peace and progress for all" (UN 2020). In his role as the secretary-general, Guterres has continued to showcase the UN's commitment to gender equality, perhaps in response to the growing expectation of international civil society organizations. Notwithstanding, a woman has yet to be selected to the highest office within the UN system. The failure to appoint a woman in 2016 as the secretary-general was described by a scholar and former UN Women's chief advisor on peace and security Anne Marie Goetz (2016) as "a stark illustration of how male-dominated decision-making means that female leadership is not just rare, but virtually inconceivable." Most recently, Guterres secured reappointment for the second term, now to head the UN until the end of 2026.

Thirdly and finally, WPS resolutions brought before the Security Council in 2019 and 2020 manifested a growing resistance or even a backlash against gender equality and women's rights within the Security Council. Passed in April 2019, UNSCR 2467 sparked a new debate with high relevance to gender equality and quickly became the most controversial of the WPS resolutions, dividing both the Security Council's members, international civil society organizations and scholars of WPS (cf. Davies and True 2019; Allen and Shepherd 2019; Chinkin and Rees 2019). UNSCR 2467 was the first WPS resolution that failed to be unanimously adopted. With several explicit mentions of gender equality, the gender analysis on which UNSCR 2467 rests is solid. The resolution noted that the goals of women's participation and protection "are inextricably linked and mutually-reinforcing," stating that "advancing gender equality and women's political, social and economic empowerment is critical to the prevention of and response to sexual violence in conflict and post-conflict situations" (S/RES/2467, preamble). Most significantly, the resolution adopted "a survivor-centred approach in preventing and responding to sexual violence in conflict and post-conflict situations" (S/RES/2467, OP 16). This has been a remarkable development in the context of the Security Council that had historically shown little appreciation of issues around personal security and safety. Despite the narrow focus on conflict-related sexual violence in UNSCR 2467, a survivor-centered approach prioritized the rights of women and other victims over national and global security interests. Ultimately, UNSCR 2467 reaffirmed and strengthened the human rights paradigm of gender equality.

However, just as important as what was included in UNSCR 2467 is what was left out in the process of the heated political negotiations that preceded the resolution. The initiative to convene a new institutional mechanism in the form of a Working Group on Sexual Violence in Conflict (similar to the Working Group on Children and Armed Conflict that has been in operation since 2005) was watered down by Russia and China who threatened to veto any such proposal (What's In Blue 2019). But even though the working group was not included in the final text, both countries abstained in the vote (S/PV.8514). In their statements, both Russia and China once again located the objective of gender equality outside the ambit of the Security Council. Russia asserted that "it is unacceptable to constantly promote concepts and terms that have either previously failed to achieve consensus or been rejected by the council," while China adjoined, stating, "We believe that the council should address sexual violence in conflict in line with its mandate, instead of going too far to address what should have been entrusted to other bodies" (S/PV.8514). Neither country spoke of gender equality explicitly at that time, but both rejected the key premise of the human rights paradigm of gender equality, that is, understanding that conflict-related sexual violence and gender inequalities are intrinsically linked and should be addressed as such.

This was not the only controversy pertaining to UNSCR 2467. Historically considered one of the "penholders" of the WPS agenda, the United States effectively watered down the inclusion of language on sexual and reproductive health of women affected by conflict-related sexual violence in the body of the resolution, undermining the gains of previous resolutions (especially UNSCR 1889). This is barely surprising in the era of "Trumpism" and the backlash against gender equality globally, especially in relation to women's rights, bodily autonomy, and access to multi-sectoral reproductive care (see also Allen and Shepherd 2019). After the removal of this language, the United States voted in support of UNSCR 2467. Nonetheless, the positions of the United States, Russia, and China—all three of them being permanent member states of the Security Council—sent a strong message against addressing the broad objective of gender equality within the mandate of the Security Council and against the protection of and respect for the full and equal rights, that for many are the blueprint for the WPS agenda.

A few months after the wrangle around UNSCR 2467, the Security Council adopted UNSCR 2493, the tenth resolution under the banner of WPS. UNSCR 2493 is preservative. It is the shortest of WPS resolutions and did not introduce any new provisions or deepen the understanding of gender inequalities. Instead, the goal of the resolution was reportedly to reestablish the consensus among the Security Council's members in relation to the WPS agenda that was rattled by the polarizing debate earlier that year. Gender equality was mentioned explicitly (S/RES/2493, OP 5) and the human rights language was maintained, albeit in a precautionary manner.

And yet the supposed consensus was short-lived. The twentieth anniversary of UNSCR 1325 in October 2020 marked the first resolution on WPS that failed to pass, having seen as many as ten member states of the Security Council abstaining in the vote. These ten member states[2] justified their decision by the refusal to support a resolution that could undermine the gains of the past two decades. Under the façade of addressing the impacts of COVID-19 on women, Russia put to vote a draft resolution that the majority of the Security Council's members considered as an impediment, rather than enhancement, to the full implementation of the WPS agenda. For example, both Germany and Belgium stated that should the resolution be adopted, "it would erode the hard-won gains" of previous years, the latter adding that the resolution "fails to meet the minimum standard with regard to civil society involvement and human rights" (S/2020/1076, annex 22 and 17). The United Kingdom maintained that "this draft text lacks sufficient language on implementation and fails to reflect core components of the framework, such as the essential rights-based approach and the structural barriers to gender equality" (S/2020/1076, annex 26). Estonia laid out the specific shortcomings of the resolution in this statement:

> The text inadequately reflects the foundation of international human rights law, on which the women and peace and security is based, including the Committee on the Elimination of All Forms of Discrimination Against Women General Recommendation No. 30. It fails to sufficiently address the link between the restrictions on women's full enjoyment of human rights and the challenges related to their participation and protection. It also does not address the structural barriers faced by women. (S/2020/1076, annex 20)

The attempt to contain WPS issues within a narrow and securitized frame-work and move away from the human rights tradition, as advocated within this failed resolution, would also undercut the gravity of UNSCR 1325's broad vision of gender equality on the twentieth anniversary of UNSCR 1325.

CONCLUSION

This chapter elucidated the subtleties and tensions in the operation of gender equality at the level of the UN Security Council. It singled out three distinct paradigms of gender equality within the vision of UNSCR 1325 that under-scored women's voices in peace and security, and women's experiences of armed conflict and its aftermath. By focusing on the protection of women (and children) from conflict-related sexual violence and on the inclusion of women in police and military roles, the security paradigm offered the nar-rowest idea of gender equality within the WPS agenda. The development paradigm implied a slightly broader conception through the discussion of a set of socioeconomic and health-related issues that affect gender equality and through the emphasis on women's empowerment and needs. Finally, the human rights paradigm adopted a broad outlook on gender equality, and through the attention to women's leadership and rights, it highlighted the con-tinuum of participation (between informal and formal) and violence (between structural and physical) in contexts of conflict, post-conflict, and nonconflict.

As I argued throughout this chapter, the distinction between the security, development, and human rights paradigms of gender equality is not merely the-oretical. Rather, it has had real-life implications and far-reaching consequences for the implementation practice and for the actual impact of the WPS agenda. Each of the paradigms has led to policy and institutional developments within the agenda that have produced certain opportunities and risks for a meaningful change to gender inequalities and power imbalances in peace and security.

While the development but especially the security paradigm of gender equality has proven more persuasive in the chamber of the Security Council, both of them emphasizing the benefits of gender equality, I argued that they have done little to challenge structural inequalities. Instead, the goal of gen-der equality has been easily co-opted for other objectives, be it global and national stability or reestablishment of post-conflict societies. Furthermore, the security and development paradigms have entailed the profound risks of assimilation and essentialism respectively, whereby gender equality has been integrated into the existing masculinist structure of the peace and security sector, and the gender difference has been effectively stereotyped. As such, the impact of these paradigms has been shortsighed: the quick gender equal-ity advances that they have brought about have been followed by long-term ambiguous consequences that will have to be carefully considered in the third decade of UNSCR 1325.

The human rights paradigm, the most promising one, has avoided the above risks and demonstrated the capacity to address the root causes of inequalities through a concerted effort to tackle structural issues under the leadership of women and in collaboration with civil society. Yet the human rights paradigm has been increasingly criticized by some of the Security Council's members, as most evident in 2019 and 2020. These member states include some of the permanent members of the Security Council who have the power to veto any future proposals regarding gender equality.

The trajectory of gender equality ultimately demonstrates high susceptibility to the politics of the Security Council as well as to the changing global optics. The three trends identified post-2015 and discussed in the final part of the chapter, that is, the new forms of securitization of the WPS agenda in the context of Countering Violent Extremism, the continued marginalization of women's leadership at the highest levels of the UN, and the growing resistance of the Security Council toward addressing the human rights paradigm under the council's mandate, point to the frailty of any progress toward gender equality. Critical feminist scholars noted that in global gender politics, "despite the difficulties of agenda setting, agenda keeping is the real challenge for feminist advocates" (Zwingel et al. 2014, 182). This appears to be the case of the WPS agenda as well, where the human rights tradition of UNSCR 1325 has been contested in the context of the twentieth anniversary of the resolution, despite important advances made over the years.

Yet active resistance and backlash against gender equality is also a sign that change is actually taking place (Flood et al. 2020). It signals that the targeted audience—the Security Council—is listening more carefully. In this sense, resistance can be seen as a positive development because it moves the goal of gender equality from the rhetoric to action in the context of the WPS agenda. But while backlash signifies that "changes to women's status seem possible or underway," it may result in "progress toward gender equality [being] halted, slowed or reversed" (Flood et al. 2020, 3).

The ten members of the Security Council who stood their ground and abstained in vote of the draft resolution presented on the twentieth anniversary on UNSCR 1325 protected the gains of the previous decades. It is paramount to continue to monitor the gender equality policymaking involved in the WPS agenda at the level of the Security Council with its many paradoxes, so as to ensure that the hard-won gains are not jeopardized in the third decade of UNSCR 1325. The following chapters will consider how some of the key tensions around gender equality in peace and security are negotiated at the regional and national levels, and how regional security organizations and national governments tackle the challenges embedded in the WPS agenda and (dis)engage with the different paradigms of gender equality for a plethora of reasons.

NOTES

1. The exception is "hard security"—driven thematic resolutions, such as Maintenance of International Peace and Security or on Terrorism, some of which were passed under Chapter VII.

2. That is, Belgium, the Dominican Republic, Estonia, France, Germany, Niger, the Saint Vincent and the Grenadines, Tunisia, the United Kingdom, and the United States. In favor voted: China, Russia, Indonesia, South Africa, and Viet Nam.

Chapter 2

The Association of Southeast Asian Nations and the Pacific Islands Forum

With the global diffusion of the UN's Women, Peace, and Security (WPS) agenda, the goal of gender equality in peace and security has spread beyond the UN system, interacting with regional and national institutions and politics (True 2016). The regional and national levels are where the impact of armed conflicts and security challenges is experienced most acutely (e.g., Coomaraswamy 2015). By the same token, the regional and national levels are also where the WPS agenda can lead to real-life changes toward greater gender equality. Regional organizations are major actors that can guide the implementation of the WPS agenda's objectives across a larger number of geopolitically interconnected states facing similar challenges (Hudson 2013; Davies et al. 2014). They can be carriers and promoters of UN Security Council Resolution 1325 (UNSCR 1325), which inaugurated the WPS agenda back in 2000. In doing so, regional organizations can play the crucial role of an intermediary between international and national implementation of the WPS agenda. Yet as will become clear throughout this chapter, regional organizations are not merely recipients of global discourses on gender equality in peace and security but also shape the meaning and purpose of the WPS agenda and how it informs regional and national policy and practice (see also Basu 2016a; 2016b).

This chapter explores the compliance of regional organizations with UNSCR 1325 in Asia and the Pacific. The aim of this exploration is to trace the operation of gender equality in peace and security in the region and position it vis-à-vis the global practice on the WPS agenda. The region comprises two vastly different subregions of Asia and the Pacific. The Association of Southeast Asian Nations (ASEAN) and the Pacific Islands Forum (PIF) are major political organizations in these subregions that foster regional cooperation and security. Despite the past and present history of armed conflict and ongoing peace and security efforts on the one hand and gender equality efforts on the other, both Asia and the Pacific were slower to engage with the WPS agenda when compared to other parts of the world (Barrow 2016; George 2016). The involvement of ASEAN and the PIF and their member states with UNSCR 1325 was somewhat reluctant throughout the entire first decade of the resolution. However, this skepticism toward the WPS agenda has started to change from 2010 onward (Davies and Lee-Koo 2018, 4; see also Lee-Koo and Trojanowska 2017).

Drawing on the policy analysis of the WPS agenda in ASEAN and the PIF, I was able to connect the ambiguous traction of the agenda to the regions' (dis)engagement with the paradigms of gender equality that emerged within UNSCR 1325 and subsequent resolutions. Resonating with the security, development, and human rights pillars of the UN system, the paradigms of gender equality offered a different interpretation of two central objectives of UNSCR 1325; that is, promoting women's *voices* in conflict prevention, conflict resolution, and post-conflict peacebuilding, and attending to women's *experiences* of armed conflict and insecurity.

Each paradigm implicated a distinct conception of gender equality. *The security paradigm* centered the understanding of gender equality around the protection of women (and children) from conflict-related sexual violence and the inclusion of women in police and military roles. *The development paradigm* broadened this narrow concept of gender equality to emphasize women's empowerment and needs in peace processes and peacebuilding. *The human rights paradigm* called for women's participation and leadership in all political processes and for protection from all forms of violence and violations against women's rights, demonstrating how gender equality operates on the continuum between conflict and peace.

In the context of Asia and the Pacific, I found that the security paradigm, which initially dominated the UN's peace and security discourse around gender equality, was rejected by both ASEAN and the PIF. With its emphasis on the responsibility of the international community to protect women from conflict-related sexual violence, the security paradigm was incongruent with preexisting norms in the region of Asia and the Pacific that underscored the rule of noninterference. In lieu of employing the security paradigm, ASEAN and the PIF have demonstrated their commitment to UNSCR 1325 in ways distinct from one another, engaging with the less securitized paradigms: development and human rights respectively. A cross-analysis of the gender equality trajectory in the implementation of the WPS agenda by ASEAN and the PIF elucidated the resistance toward global discourses that are sometimes perceived as a threat to regional security (see also George 2016) rather than a means to greater gender equality. The development and human rights paradigms connected better with conceptual priors regarding gender equality and fit into the regional security politics of Asia and the Pacific. While ASEAN and the PIF would repeat some of the global challenges of gender equality policymaking, such as essentializing women's roles or inadequate implementation of the WPS agenda, they have also demonstrated ways regional organizations can meaningfully connect global discourses to regional challenges.

This chapter relies on three sources of data. Policy documents developed by ASEAN and the PIF and their member states to implement the WPS agenda lay out the foundation to understand how gender equality has been approached by these organizations in relation to their peace and security efforts. This understanding is situated within broader policy environments of ASEAN and the PIF and their other gender equality and security frameworks, which provide the second source of data utilized to contextualize UNSCR 1325's objectives within regional politics. Finally, the analysis of gender equality in ASEAN and the PIF is supported by statements (where available) made during debates on WPS at the UN Security Council in which the respective organizations had an opportunity to update the council's members on the progress made at the regional level and position it in relation to global developments.

This chapter starts with outlining the rationale for regional and national implementation of UNSCR 1325 and the key role regional organizations play in these processes. In the second part, I provide the background to ASEAN's and the PIF's engagement with the WPS agenda and probe the ambiguous traction of UNSCR 135 across Asia and the Pacific, linking it to the historical and sociopolitical context of the region. The third and fourth parts interrogate the trajectory of gender equality in WPS policy of ASEAN and the PIF respectively, exploring the implementation by these organizations and by their member states, including the relationship between regional and national initiatives. I conclude the chapter with a reflection on possibilities and limitations embedded in gender equality policymaking at the juncture of the global and regional implementation of the WPS agenda at the time of increasing political instability in Asia and the Pacific.

THE ROLE OF REGIONAL ORGANIZATIONS IN IMPLEMENTING UNSCR 1325

Regional and national engagement with UNSCR 1325 is paramount to meeting the WPS agenda's objectives and bringing about real-life changes to gender inequalities and power imbalances involved in peace and security (True 2016; Swaine 2017; Coomaraswamy 2015). In other words, UNSCR 1325 must reach beyond the UN Headquarters and connect with local realities of populations affected by conflict and post-conflict situations in order to influence the goal of gender equality in peace and security more directly (Coomaraswamy 2015). In recognition of the importance of WPS localization, a dozen regional organizations and just over half of UN member states across Europe, Africa, the Americas (particularly North America), and later Asia and the Pacific have launched specific frameworks to guide the implementation of the WPS agenda in contexts where conflicts occur (PeaceWomen 2021).

The development of regional and national frameworks has become the most common form of compliance with UNSCR 1325 outside the UN system (Swaine 2017; Fritz et al. 2011; Trojanowska et al. 2018). These frameworks, primarily regional action plans (RAPs) and national action plans (NAPs), have provided a vehicle to apply the objectives of the WPS agenda to specific geopolitical locations, accounting for regional differences and national priorities (True 2016). In a nutshell, action plans stipulate a policy or strategic directions of a regional organization (in the case of RAPs) or a national government (in the case of NAPs) with respect to the WPS agenda (see also Miller et al. 2014, 10). In terms of the scope, this policy or strategy may be domestic and/or foreign, and action plans are divided into inward- and outward-looking accordingly (Shepherd 2016). In terms of the mechanics, action plans are typically two-part documents comprising a narrative report (outlining the specific situation, security challenges, and their gender-differentiated impact, and the relevance of UNSCR 1325 to that context) as well as an implementation matrix (including activities, monitoring indicators, reporting schema, and governance structure) (e.g., George et al. 2019). The primary difference between RAPs and NAPs is that while both provide implementation guidelines for specific actors, RAPs express collective views of the broader membership of a regional organization, while NAPs are limited to the perspective of the government in question (Hudson 2013). Globally, NAPs predated RAPs by a few years and have been more prominent.

The encouragement toward the adoption of national-level policies on UNSCR 1325 and NAPs came from the UN Security Council and the UN secretary-general as early as 2002 and 2004 (see S/PRST/2002/32 and S/2004/814, para. 4–5). National efforts of UN member states to develop NAPs were subsequently recognized in WPS resolutions (e.g., S/RES/1889, preamble; S/RES/2122, preamble; S/RES/2242, OP 2). The UN-sponsored *Global Study on the Implementation of United Nations Security Council Resolution 1325*, which evaluated the progress between 2000 and 2015 across the globe, explicitly stated that "nation states remain the most influential actors in the implementation of the WPS agenda" (Coomaraswamy 2015, 240), while one of the most recent resolutions called for a sustained commitment to NAPs, encouraging UN member states to fund and regularly refresh their plans (S/RES/2467, OP 35).

As of late 2021, the totality of ninety-eight member states, or close to 51 percent of all UN member states, launched NAPs (PeaceWomen 2021). European countries such as Denmark, Sweden, Norway, and the United Kingdom led the early adoption of NAPs starting in 2005 and 2006, despite no recent history of armed conflict on their territory. These NAPs were predominantly outward-focused and engaged the WPS agenda in peacekeeping efforts in conflict-ridden parts of the world. Beginning in 2008 and 2009, inward-focused NAPs were developed in conflict-affected countries of Africa and Latin America, including in Cote d'Ivoire, Uganda, Liberia, and Chile. The Philippines and Nepal pioneered NAPs in Asia and the Pacific in 2010 and 2011. These NAPs typically addressed domestic challenges related to gender equality, conflict, and insecurity. The United States and Australia also launched their plans, in 2011 and 2012 respectively (PeaceWomen 2021). It is worth noting that several of these countries adopted further iterations of NAPs to renew commitments and account for changes in the political landscape, including issues of violent extremism and the COVID-19 pandemic (see S/2020/946, para. 79).

RAPs, even though less prominent than NAPs, have also been encouraged by the UN system. WPS resolutions included multiple references to regional organizations' involvement in the implementation of UNSCR 1325 (S/RES/1820, OP 14) emphasizing their "important complementary role" to efforts by UN agencies and governments (S/RES/2467, preamble; S/RES/2493, preamble). Some resolutions specifically urged the development of RAPs (e.g., S/RES/2122, preamble; S/RES/2242, OP 2). Since 2008, eleven regional organizations released their regional policies on WPS in the form of RAPs (PeaceWomen 2021). These are: the Southern African Development Community, the East African Community, the Economic Community of West African States, the European Union, the North Atlantic Treaty Organization, the Pacific Islands Forum, the African Union, the International Conference on the Great Lakes Region, the Organization for Security and Cooperation in Europe, the League of Arab States, and the Intergovernmental Authority on Development (S/2018/900, para. 53). Just like NAPs, some RAPs have been updated over time and followed by further iterations.

While NAPs have become the major mechanism for the institutionalization and implementation of the WPS agenda beyond the UN system (True 2016; Swaine 2009; 2017; Tryggestad 2014; Barrow 2016; Trojanowska et al. 2018), RAPs and NAPs can be both complementary and mutually reinforcing (Coomaraswamy 2015, 257; Hudson 2013). A growing body of scholarly and practitioner literature on WPS underscored the importance of regional organizations, and RAPs have been acknowledged as "a critical tool in implementing the WPS resolutions given the cross-border impact of many contemporary armed conflicts today" (Hudson 2013, 11; see also Hamilton et al. 2020). Researchers identified multiple advantages of RAPs, whether operational—such as sharing expertise and lessons learned between states as well as mobilizing resources for the implementation of UNSCR 1325—or normative—such as applying a positive pressure on states in a given region to engage with the WPS agenda through national policies and laws (Davies et al. 2014, 346). There is evidence that regional organizations and regional frameworks have enabled national implementation of the WPS agenda, serving as an impetus for the adoption of NAPs. Coomaraswamy (2015, 257) found such positive influence in the Economic Community of West African States, where twelve out of fifteen member states developed their NAPs following the release of the RAP. This trend will be also noted, albeit to a lesser extent, in the case of the PIF. Conversely, the adoption of NAPs can pivot the development of a regional policy, as in the example of ASEAN, where national frameworks adopted by some of the member states of the regional organization influenced its commitment to the WPS agenda, as will be discussed later in this chapter. Before delving into the case studies of the PIF and ASEAN, the following section will outline the sociopolitical context to WPS implementation in Asia and the Pacific and situate the regional organizations' engagement with UNSCR 1325 within it.

THE ENGAGEMENT OF ASIA AND THE PACIFIC WITH THE WOMEN, PEACE, AND SECURITY AGENDA

With NAPs and RAPs proliferating across the globe, Asia and the Pacific were initially missing from this WPS story (Basu 2016a; 2016b; Lee-Koo and Trojanowska 2017). Asia and the Pacific was the last major geographical region to comply with UNSCR 1325 through the development of dedicated policies. Researchers noted that states in the region were "slower to recognise the importance of this [WPS] agenda" (George 2016, 376), and the adoption of NAPs "lagged behind" in comparison with other parts of the world (Barrow 2016, 24). The same can be said about regional organizations' involvement in the WPS agenda, especially the major security organization ASEAN (Davies et al. 2014). In more recent years, however, the WPS agenda has gained prominence in the region and Davies and Lee-Koo (2018, 4) noted that "Asia and the Pacific have established significant momentum in the implementation of the WPS agenda" (see also Swaine 2016). The positionality of the WPS agenda vis-à-vis the historical context of Asia and the Pacific helps understand the initial resistance toward UNSCR 1325 and what has changed over time, linking the WPS traction to the understanding of gender equality.

The instability of Asia and the Pacific and multiple gender inequalities that exist in the region, often exacerbated by conflict and insecurity, suggest that UNSCR 1325 is pertinent to this regional context. Plagued by armed conflicts and prolonged violence, natural disasters, and growing incidences of violent extremism, Asia and the Pacific comprises arguably one of the most insecure regions for the inhabitants (D'Costa and Lee-Koo 2009). Many states are politically unstable, continuing to emerge from security crises, and the vulnerability of conflict-affected populations has been compounded by the COVID-19 pandemic (Gordon 2020).

Cambodia, Indonesia, Myanmar, Nepal, the Philippines, Sri Lanka, and Timor Leste have all suffered from recent inter- and intra-state conflicts, while the Republic of Korea remains the only country in the world under an active armistice agreement (UCDP n.d.b; see also Barrow 2016). The Pacific Islands have also experienced several protracted conflicts, including the intertribal violence in the Solomon Islands, the rebel insurgency in Fiji, and the Bougainvillean struggle for autonomy from Papua New Guinea (e.g., George 2014). The colonial history of nuclear testing has led to the degradation of natural resources in the Pacific Islands, endangering not only regional but also global environmental security (George 2014) and making the region more prone to intrastate violence (Bhagwan-Rolls 2014). Furthermore, South East Asia has seen multiple events that have shaken the stability of the region and the world just over the past few years, such as the military crisis and ethnic cleansing in Rakhine State, Myanmar; the nuclear threat posed by the precarious relationship between the United States and North Korea; the growing radicalization of foreign fighters in Indonesia; and the declaration of martial law followed by mass human rights abuses in Mindanao, the Philippines, to name a few (Human Rights Watch 2018; 2019; 2020). As aptly summarized by critical researchers of security, Asia and the Pacific remain "one of the most dynamic, challenging and . . . potentially threatening regions of the world" (D'Costa and Lee-Koo 2009, 4; see also McDonald 2017).

Armed conflicts and security challenges across Asia and the Pacific have had pervasive gender effects. Women and girls in particular have been affected in a number of ways: "whether as survivors of gender-based violence, through internal displacement and economic dislocation, as refugees or as combatants in insurgency movements" (Barrow 2016, 24–25). The instability of the region has not only threatened women's security and hindered their political participation but also mobilized them to take part in peacebuilding activities or to join armed struggles. Indeed, women have played an active role in all these conflicts and civil wars in Asia and the Pacific (Davies et al. 2014; George 2014; Bhagwan-Rolls 2014). The region of Asia and the Pacific is therefore characterized by gender paradoxes, whereby multiple sources of opportunity for women coexist with great gender disparities and gender-based violence (D'Costa and Lee-Koo 2009).

Despite the relevance of UNSCR 1325 to the sociopolitical context and despite the preexisting efforts toward gender equality, Asia and the Pacific did not engage with the WPS agenda at the outset (Barrow 2016). It is important to note that the countries of Asia and the Pacific—such as Bangladesh, India, Pakistan, and Indonesia—are among the highest police and military troop contributors to UN operations (UNDPO 2021), which is an additional imperative to the implementation of the WPS agenda. And yet little evidence of regional and national interest in the agenda in Asia and the Pacific can be established throughout the entire first decade of UNSCR 1325. However, this started to change around 2010 and the WPS agenda has gradually gained traction in the region (see also Lee-Koo and Trojanowska 2017). Ten governments released their NAPs (chronologically): the Philippines, Nepal, Australia, the Republic of Korea, Indonesia, New Zealand, Japan, Timor Leste, the Solomon Islands, and Bangladesh, while Bougainville and Thailand developed specific guidelines and policies relating to WPS. Moreover, the PIF launched a RAP and ASEAN committed to UNSCR 1325 through an official statement cosigned by all member states (PeaceWomen 2021; see also LSE and USYD n.d.).

The initial delay in implementing the WPS agenda should be situated within the historical resistance of Asia and the Pacific toward the UN system and global discourses that are often incongruent with regional politics (Nasu 2011; Rajan and Desai 2013). UN-led processes can be perceived in Asia and the Pacific to be a "threat" to regional security rather than a solution to global insecurity (George 2014). This is because global frameworks originating from the UN system are sometimes associated with imperialist and neo-colonial tendencies of powerful member states of the UN Security Council. Those actors have been accused of using the safety, well-being, and rights of women to expand their political influences and enlarge economic gains, with such tendencies being identified also with respect to UNSCR 1325 (e.g., Pratt 2013; Shepherd 2016).

Relatedly, preexisting norms developed in Asia and the Pacific, such as noninterference or avoidance of military pacts, emphasize sovereignty most strongly (Acharya 2005). National autonomy is valued over collective decision-making, and this has resulted in additional contention of global security frameworks, for example, Humanitarian Intervention or Responsibility to Protect. Both frameworks called on the international community to intervene, including through the use of military force, when states fail to address gross human rights violations or protect their populations from mass atrocities (UN 2005; see also Acharya 2004; Bellamy and Beeson 2010; Bellamy and Davies 2009).

In terms of the WPS agenda, the skepticism toward the security paradigm of gender equality would be pronounced in Asia and the Pacific. The security paradigm dominated global debates around gender equality in peace and security at least until 2015, gaining significant support both from the UN Security Council and agencies such as the UN Department of Peace Operations. Essentially, the security paradigm focused on issues of conflict-related sexual violence. The Security Council's resolutions that operationalized the security paradigm put in place some protection measures, among others urging the use of targeted sanctions in contexts where sexual violence has been used strategically as a weapon of warfare (e.g., S/RES/2106, OP 13; Huvé 2018; for more, see chapter 1). Additionally, the resolutions encouraged the inclusion of women in the security sector to combat this problem (e.g., S/RES/1960, preamble; S/RES/1888, preamble). Efforts toward gender equality were ultimately conceived as a means to security-driven ends. Such securitized approaches to gender equality have proven to be incompatible with regional security politics, colliding with the preexisting rule of noninterference into national politics of states (Acharya 2004; 2005; Bellamy and Beeson 2010; Bellamy and Davies 2009). They have also clashed with regional conceptions of gender equality that tend to emphasize women's roles in peacebuilding and post-conflict recovery rather than sexual violence and the participation of women in military and police roles (Davies 2016).

The global prominence of the security paradigm throughout the first decade of UNSCR 1325 subsequently discouraged regional involvement in WPS implementation, accounting—at least in part—for the limited engagement of Asia and the Pacific with UNSCR 1325 and subsequent resolutions. The other paradigms of gender equality that emerged in the global WPS agenda in later years, that is, development and human rights, resonated better with regional politics and conceptual priors in Asia and the Pacific. They have also been followed by substantive interest in the WPS agenda observed in the region since 2010, as will be discussed in the following in relation to ASEAN and the PIF and their member states.

ASSOCIATION OF SOUTHEAST ASIAN NATIONS

ASEAN is a major security organization in Asia (Acharya 2004; Davies 2017). Formed in 1967 by Indonesia, Malaysia, the Philippines, Singapore, and Thailand, ASEAN was joined by Brunei Darussalam, Viet Nam, Laos, Cambodia, and Myanmar in the 1990s (ASEAN n.d.). Given its important role in regional security politics, ASEAN is well placed to advocate for the implementation of global frameworks such as the UN's WPS agenda.

Researchers and activists alike suggested that "there is both a practical and normative need for ASEAN—through its member states—to give an express commitment to UNSC Resolution 1325" (Davies et al. 2014, 335; Sloane 2017; Nair 2018; Davies and Lee-Koo 2018). Yet the organization demonstrated little interest in pursuing the WPS agenda until 2017. Similarly, the engagement of ASEAN's member states has been quite limited, with only two (out of ten) countries having adopted NAPs thus far, namely the Philippines and Indonesia, while Thailand developed national guidelines on WPS that do not constitute a NAP. The resistance toward securitized notions of gender equality has been evident in ASEAN, which would instead emphasize women's contributions to peacebuilding and post-conflict relief and recovery, and would eventually adopt the development paradigm of gender equality in its emerging regional WPS policy.

The security paradigm of gender equality advocated at the level of the UN Security Council has been incongruent with the security and gender equality politics of ASEAN as well as with its institutional structure, resulting in limited traction of UNSCR 1325. Starting with the regional security politics, the skepticism of ASEAN toward the WPS agenda was evident in the lack of engagement of the organization with the UN Security Council on these issues in early years of UNSCR 1325. For example, ASEAN refrained from delivering statements at most of the Security Council's annual debates on WPS until about 2015. Such statements were commonly presented by other regional organizations, such as the European Union. At the UN Security Council High-Level Review of Women, Peace, and Security in October 2015, Viet Nam eventually delivered a statement on behalf of ASEAN that outlined the position of this regional organisation by stating that "special emphasis must be placed on respect for the sovereignty, territorial integrity, and political independence of States, on refraining from the threat of or use of force and on the settlement of disputes by peaceful means" (S/PV.7533, Resumption 1). This is in line with the political culture of ASEAN as well as the preexisting norms discussed earlier in this chapter, which underscored national autonomy and nonintervention. ASEAN's statement, while recognizing in other places the important role of the international community and regional organizations in implementing the WPS agenda, discouraged securitized approaches to gender equality, peace, and security.

The security paradigm further failed to resonate with predating notions of gender equality in ASEAN that envisaged this policy goal as a development (or less commonly, human rights) issue rather than a security matter. In this context, the limited traction of UNSCR 1325 in ASEAN's politics contrasts with important policy developments within the organizations pertaining to gender equality. Since the late 1980s, ASEAN introduced several policies and frameworks related to gender equality. They include, among others:

the Declaration of the Advancement of Women in the ASEAN Region (1988), the Declaration on the Elimination of Violence against Women in the ASEAN Region (2004), the Ha Noi Declaration on the Enhancement of the Welfare and Development of ASEAN Women and Children (2010), the ASEAN Human Rights Declaration (2012), the Declaration on the Elimination of Violence Against Women and Elimination of Violence against Children (2013), the ASEAN Convention against Trafficking in Persons, Especially Women and Children (2015), and the ASEAN Declaration on the Gender-Responsive Implementation of the ASEAN Community Vision 2025 and Sustainable Development Goals (2017) (for more, see ASEAN n.d.). Despite the fact that most of these policies were drafted after the adoption of UNSCR 1325 and many explicitly mentioned the situation of women affected by conflict, few referenced the WPS agenda on any occasion.

As early as 1988, the Declaration of the Advancement of Women in the ASEAN Region stipulated that the organization shall endeavor:

> To enable women in the region to undertake their important role as active agents and beneficiaries of national and regional development, particularly in promoting regional understanding and cooperation and in building more just and peaceful societies. (ASEAN 1988, OP 2)

The declaration recognized the role of women in peacebuilding and development, and it did so over a decade prior to UNSCR 1325. The current ASEAN Regional Plan of Action on the Elimination of Violence against Women (2016-2025) failed to meaningfully engage with WPS as well, limiting the recognition of UNSCR 1325 to a single preambulatory paragraph with no concrete meaning or associated call for action (ASEAN 2015, preamble).

Earlier frameworks conceived gender equality as a means to the development and economy of member states of ASEAN. As such, the pursuit of gender equality has been embedded in a set of gender-stereotyping assumptions about the role of women in society. Davies (2016, 119 and 106) similarly maintained that ASEAN's commitments to women were "framed by a developmental approach," locating ASEAN's "failure to engage with the WPS agenda in a particular elite understanding of women as both non-political and vehicles for the realisation of economic and social well-being." Such an approach entailed the commonplace risk of many gender equality policies adopted globally that essentialize the gender difference and attribute certain qualities, typically caretaking, to women. By fulfilling gender-stereotyped roles, women are expected to contribute to families' and communities' welfare and by extension to post-conflict nations' economies. The meaning and purpose of gender equality are ultimately depoliticized.

Finally, the institutional structure of ASEAN supported the understanding of gender equality as a non-security issue, again discouraging the early engagement with UNSCR 1325 (Davies et al. 2014, 354–355). ASEAN operates across three priority areas: political-security community, economic community, and sociocultural community (ASEAN n.d.). Gender equality has been traditionally addressed within economic and especially sociocultural communities. Political-security community, which deals with high-level security politics and is perhaps the most important pillar of ASEAN, rarely engages with women's or equality issues. The discussion of UNSCR 1325 has also been predominantly located in those less influential priority areas of ASEAN. When it comes to political-security community, research by Davies and colleagues (2014) demonstrated that the rare and passing references to the WPS agenda failed to link violence against women and regional and global security, as was envisaged in the global security paradigm of gender equality.

With the broadening of the UN's peace and security discourse toward other conceptions of gender equality came WPS developments within ASEAN. The organization's concern with UNSCR 1325 would be evident from 2017 onward. Most significantly, in November 2017 in Manila, the Philippines, the member states of ASEAN signed the Joint Statement on Promoting Women, Peace, and Security (ASEAN 2017). The statement is merely a two-page document, but it is important to note because it was the first explicit and public indication of ASEAN's political and organizational will to implement the WPS agenda through its structure and membership. The statement situates the WPS agenda at the juncture of earlier commitments of ASEAN to "promote regional peace and stability and sustainable development" as well as to "ensure gender equality and empowerment of women" (ASEAN 2017). Despite being rather generic, the statement embeds the major elements of the global WPS agenda around the gender-differentiated impact of armed conflicts on women and the role that women can play in peacebuilding and post-conflict reconstruction.

Gender equality is addressed explicitly in two operative paragraphs that call on the member states of ASEAN to "promote gender equality and reduce social inequalities between men and women in our societies as a way to contribute as well to long-standing peace and prosperity" and to "continue addressing the root causes of armed conflicts such as poverty, discrimination, gender inequality, social injustice, economic and social exclusion of persons and communities vulnerable to and at risk of radicalization, violent extremism and terrorism" (ASEAN 2017). Again, the socioeconomic aspects of gender equality are emphasized most strongly, and the objective appears to be perceived through the development lens, whereby women's empowerment and participation in peace processes is a means to sustainable peace and development. The statement delivered by ASEAN at the Security Council's debate on WPS in 2018 reaffirmed this perspective on the WPS agenda and ASEAN's commitment to "the promotion of gender equality and women's empowerment as a means of contributing to long-lasting peace and prosperity" (S/PV.8382).

ASEAN has continued to engage with the WPS agenda in following years and has seen important developments (see also Heyzer 2020). In 2018, the ASEAN Women and Peace Registry was established to gather information about women peace leaders across the region with expertise in peace and security (S/PV.8649, resumption 2). Moreover, the 26th ASEAN Regional Forum held in August 2019 in Bangkok, Thailand, resulted in the adoption of the Joint Statement on Promoting the Women, Peace, and Security Agenda (ASEAN Regional Forum 2019) by ASEAN member states in collaboration with other members of the ASEAN Regional Forum.[1] In the same month, ASEAN convened its first Regional Symposium on Implementing Women, Peace, and Security Agenda, wherein the organization pledged to further action on the WPS agenda. This growing commitment of ASEAN was recognized by the UN system, and the 2020 Report of the Secretary-General on Women, Peace, and Security highlighted that "[s]trengthened partnerships between the United Nations and regional organizations are essential, and the commitment by the Association of Southeast Asian Nations (ASEAN) to give greater prominence to the agenda is welcome" (S/2020/946, para. 80). While a RAP is yet to be seen, in early 2021 ASEAN released the first *ASEAN Regional Study on Women, Peace, and Security*, in which the ASEAN secretary-general, Dato Lim Jock Hoi, articulated a clear commitment to developing a regional plan of action on WPS in the near future (ASEAN 2021, IV).

National Implementation

Resistance toward securitized notions of gender equality can be noted not only in ASEAN's involvement in the WPS agenda but also in the engagement (or lack thereof) of ASEAN's member states. As of late 2021, out of the ten member states of ASEAN, only the Philippines and Indonesia adopted WPS NAPs (PeaceWomen 2021), while Thailand developed national guidelines on WPS in 2016 (Davies and Lee-Koo 2018, 11), but these guidelines do not constitute a NAP (Hamilton et al. 2020). Both the Philippines and Indonesia rejected the security paradigm of gender equality in their WPS policies. Other than this, however, their NAPs are quite different from one another in how they envisaged gender equality: through a human rights and development lens respectively.

The Philippines has over the years built the reputation of a regional and, to some extent, global WPS champion (Barrow 2016; Veneracion-Rallonza

2013; Coomaraswamy 2015; Trojanowska 2021). The country pioneered NAPs in the entire region of Asia and the Pacific with the 2010 adoption of "The Philippine National Action Plan on UNSCRs 1325 & 1820" (Government of the Philippines 2010). Since then, the government of the Philippines delivered two further iterations, launched in 2014 and 2017 (Government of the Philippines 2014; 2017). These NAPs are inward-looking and address the intrastate conflicts that have plagued the Philippines at least since the 1960s, relating in particular to the government's fights with the Moro Islamic Liberation Front and with the Communist Party of the Philippines. Founded on a rather comprehensive gender analysis of human rights abuses and violations, the NAPs demonstrated a nuanced understanding of how the rights and safety of women have been impacted directly and indirectly by conflicts and militarization in the Philippines. Over the years, the engagement with the human rights paradigm of gender equality has become more explicit. The most recent iteration pictured the Philippine WPS policy as "an articulation of women's human rights in armed conflict situations" (Government of the Philippines 2017, 10).

Importantly, the nuanced understanding of issues of gender equality in peace and security in the Philippine NAPs, embedded in local challenges, has been followed by a robust implementation strategy. The implementation framework outlined dedicated activities, responsibilities and roles, and monitoring and evaluation measures to track progress over time, aligning with the human rights principles. All of this makes the Philippines a strong case study of WPS policy and practice guided by the human rights paradigm of gender equality. Chapter 3 will be fully dedicated to this case study to elaborate on the implementation of the WPS agenda by the government of the Philippines and investigate how the human rights paradigm of gender equality can be applied to conflict and post-conflict situations and, further, how it can translate from policy to implementation practice of government departments.

The government of Indonesia's involvement in the WPS agenda was more peculiar and somewhat confusing. Launched in 2014 and now concluded, "National Action Plan for the Protection and Empowerment of Women and Children during Social Conflicts" (Government of Indonesia 2014) was devoid of explicit references to UNSCR 1325, as it was a reflection on the history or implications of armed conflicts. Indonesia experienced major and relatively recent conflicts that include especially its occupation of Timor Leste (1975–1999) and three-decade-long internal conflict between the government and the Free Aceh Movement (1976–2005) (Lee-Koo 2012). And yet the NAP remained silent about the legacy of these conflicts and the security challenges that followed, including the increasing threats posed by violent extremism (True and Eddyono 2017). According to a local activist, this was justified by the decision of the Indonesian Ministry of Foreign

Affairs to avoid the association of Indonesia's implementation of the WPS agenda with armed conflict (Kholifah 2014). Instead, the NAP of Indonesia was dedicated to community violence. It may well be the only NAP globally that refrained from mentioning UNSCR 1325 or the WPS agenda in any place, despite clearly aligning with WPS pillars of participation, protection, prevention, and relief/recovery.

With the focus on "social conflicts"—referring to community violence—the NAP of Indonesia emphasized two major issues: women's contributions to peacebuilding and sustainable development through community work on the one hand, and gender-differentiated needs of women in fragile contexts on the other. Both resonated with the features of the development paradigm of gender equality identified at the global level. As a matter of fact, Indonesia can be seen as a stark example of that paradigm with its opportunities and risks. In terms of the former, the NAP paid significant attention to women's needs in post-conflict situations, be they immediate recovery needs (such as food, clothing, shelter, needs related to menstruation, pregnancy, child delivery, or breastfeeding) or socioeconomic needs (including education and health). In doing so, this WPS policy was embedded in the local context and informed by the lived realities of women, including the social and economic challenges faced by them on a daily basis. However, this grounded approach to gender-differentiated needs of women was followed by the essentializing of women's roles, the major risk of the development paradigm. The NAP supported women in undertaking strikingly gender-stereotyped activities, such as "snack making, beauty/hair salon, bridal makeup, sewing, food stalls, handicrafts, ornamental plants, and other" (Government of Indonesia 2014, 12). This discourse and practice located women in the food, garment, beauty, and decoration industries, but even more importantly the emphasis was on women's labor and women's contributions to the national economy rather than on their political participation, rights, or well-being. Such approaches push women into neoliberal market economies, which rest on gender and other inequalities (Krook and True 2012, 116). Consequently, the NAP of Indonesia provides an example in which the development paradigm essentialized the gender difference and simultaneously depoliticized the goal of gender equality, making it merely a means to development-driven ends.

It deserves to be noted that the NAP of Indonesia presented a relatively strong implementation framework. The implementation strategy bore marks of the grounded approach to WPS implementation and also of depoliticization of gender equality. Overall, the NAP designed a multilevel governance mechanism with responsibilities assigned to officials at national, district, and provincial levels. It also developed a highly specific implementation matrix with action points and corresponding indicators. These actions were concrete and implementable, and the indicators were targeted and specific. However, some of them were irrelevant, such as the indicator related to the "percentage of cities with green open space," which has little to do with gender equality in peace and security. In all of this, the NAP of Indonesia can be seen as a policy that can be effectively implemented thanks to institutional structure in place, and yet its capacity to support the political struggle for gender equality in meaningful ways can be questioned due to the problematic conceptualization of gender equality.

Lastly, the recent involvement of Indonesia in the WPS agenda at the level of the Security Council warrants a word of comment. As a member state of the UN Security Council in the years 2019–2020, Indonesia led the drafting of a resolution on women's participation in UN peacekeeping, UNSCR 2538, adopted in August 2020 under another agenda of the Security Council, namely United Nations Peacekeeping Operations. Indonesia's leadership on this issue is commended given that the country is among the major troop and police contributors to UN peace operations (see UNDPO 2021). The recognition of "the indispensable role of women in United Nations peacekeeping" (S/RES/2538, preamble) is therefore welcomed. However, merely a couple of months later, Indonesia was one of only five member states of the Security Council that voted in favor of a controversial draft resolution on WPS presented by Russia (see chapter 1). The resolution failed to pass, with as many as ten countries abstaining in the vote and claiming it would be a setback to the achievements of previous years and especially to the goals of gender equality and women's rights (S/2020/1076). Overall, the steps undertaken by Indonesia in relation to the WPS agenda have been inconsistent. It appears that gender equality has been treated as a secondary and somewhat inferior objective that has been motivated by other political priorities that have driven the implementation of UNSCR 1325 by the government of Indonesia.

Just like ASEAN, its member states saw limited engagement with the WPS agenda, despite other forms of commitment to gender equality. All ten members of ASEAN ratified the Convention on the Elimination of All Forms of Discrimination Against Women (CEDAW), the major international bill of women's rights. While Thailand developed guidelines on WPS that integrated UNSCR 1325 under preexisting gender equality frameworks (Hamilton et al. 2020), countries such as Cambodia and Myanmar launched other policies that align with WPS principles pertaining to the advancement of women and prevention of violence against women (see also Veneracion-Rallonza 2019). For the most part, national efforts toward gender equality predated and influenced ASEAN's recent engagement with UNSCR 1325 (see also Davies and Lee-Koo 2018, 6), with the countries carefully selecting approaches that suit their gender equality priorities as well as other political endeavors. The case of the PIF and its member states that I turn to now would be quite different, as the regional policy on WPS would support national implementation.

PACIFIC ISLANDS FORUM

Founded in 1971 by then newly independent Pacific states, the PIF is envisaged as a platform "to stimulate economic growth and enhance political governance and security for the region" (PIF n.d.). It now comprises fourteen sovereign Pacific countries (i.e., Cook Islands, Federated States of Micronesia, Fiji, Kiribati, Nauru, Niue, Palau, Papua New Guinea, Republic of Marshall Islands, Samoa, Solomon Islands, Tonga, Tuvalu, and Vanuatu), along with Australia and New Zealand, which joined the organization in 1999 (see also George 2016). Even though the PIF is much less powerful than ASEAN in regional and global security politics, in contrast to ASEAN's limited involvement in the WPS agenda until most recent years, it demonstrated a commitment to UNSCR 1325 with the adoption of a RAP as early as in 2012. The PIF's engagement with the WPS agenda has also been marked by the resistance toward the securitized notions of gender equality, but the organization would place at the center stage women's decision-making at all levels of peace and security and protection from all forms of women's rights violations, in line with the global human rights paradigm of gender equality.

The launch of the "Pacific Regional Action Plan on Women, Peace, and Security" (PIF 2012), or the Pacific RAP for short, had been preceded by long-standing WPS advocacy by local civil society and women peace activists in particular (Bhagwan-Rolls and Rolls 2019). This advocacy has been driven by the fact that preexisting peace and security frameworks overlooked women's voices and their experiences of armed conflict and insecurity across the Pacific Islands nearly altogether. The prime peace and security policy document, the Biketawa Declaration (PIF 2000) all but ignored the importance of gender equality (see also George 2016). The adoption of the Biketawa Declaration was a milestone for regional cooperation and security of members of the PIF and yet, with the exception of a singular reference to "gender" and "equal rights," it paid no attention to how gender equality issues interplay with armed conflict and security challenges in the region (PIF 2000, art. 1.ii). For women peace activists who mobilized under the banner of Pacific PeaceWomen, UNSCR 1325 provided an opportunity to rectify this shortcoming. In the words of Bhagwan-Rolls and Stone (2016, 87), the resolution "'licensed' Pacific women peacebuilders to demonstrate the relevance of their needs to the male-dominated political establishment." After a decade-long advocacy, the PIF eventually formed the Pacific Regional Working Group on Women, Peace, and Security in 2010 with a task to develop a regional framework for WPS implementation (Bhagwan-Rolls 2014). Comprising members from the PIF, the Council of Regional Organizations in the Pacific, the UN, and civil society organizations—particularly FemLINKPACIFIC, who drove this work (see also FemLINKPACIFIC n.d.)—the Pacific Regional Working

Group on Women, Peace, and Security drafted in a collaborative process a regional policy on WPS in the form of the Pacific RAP, released in October 2012 (see also Bhagwan-Rolls and Stone 2016; Bhagwan-Rolls and Rolls 2019).

Envisioned as a corrective to preexisting regional and national policy frameworks on peace and security, the Pacific RAP provided a means to address the gender equality gap precisely through engaging women's human rights discourse. The human rights paradigm of gender equality was evident in this regional WPS policy. The RAP started with a nuanced analysis of conflicts and security challenges across the Pacific Islands, reflecting on their gender implications. Women's leadership and women and girls' human rights remained central to this policy. Through three priority areas, the RAP committed to "women's leadership in conflict prevention and management, political decision-making and peacebuilding and peacekeeping," "women's participation in security sector oversight and accountability," and "protection of women's human rights in transitional and post-conflict contexts" (PIF 2012, 16–19).

Furthermore, the Pacific RAP demonstrated a holistic understanding of the WPS agenda and how it operates on the continuum between conflict, post-conflict, and nonconflict. Praised in WPS research (see Bhagwan-Rolls 2014), the RAP addressed a spectrum of situations whether "conflict/post-conflict, transitional contexts and humanitarian settings" or "peacebuilding and conflict prevention" (PIF 2012, 14). It is worth noting that the RAP was criticized for failing to engage with issues relating to climate change and militarization, both of which make the Pacific Islands prone to prolonged armed violence (George 2014, 326). However, the emphasis on women's leadership and rights, the comprehensive gender analysis, and the understanding of gender inequalities as occurring on a continuum provided the foundation for a solid regional WPS policy.

The strengths of the Pacific RAP are also noticeable in the implementation framework that was developed to operationalize the three focus areas. The framework stipulated the role of the RAP and parameters within which it was to operate in the PIF, firmly embedding WPS in the preexisting institutional structure. This was followed by an action matrix, inclusive of activities, responsibilities (shared between the PIF, UN agencies, and FemLINKPACIFIC), and monitoring and evaluation indicators with timeframes. With all these elements in place, the Pacific RAP presented a relatively robust framework on WPS that could be effectively implemented. Sadly, however, no funding was allocated to the implementation of the Pacific RAP at the time of its adoption, which contributed to limited action in the following years.

Indeed, there is little evidence of the implementation of the Pacific RAP. It appears that the promising discourse immersed in human rights principles and the well-thought implementation strategy did not translate into practice. The RAP spanned over three years and concluded in 2015. In the absence of any publicly available monitoring report, the impact of the Pacific RAP is—at best—unknown. What is known in the emerging literature, however, is changes to the leadership of the PIF and new restrictions on civil society engagement that led the development of the Pacific RAP in the first place. According to Bhagwan-Rolls and Stone (2016, 91; see also Bhagwan-Rolls and Rolls 2019), all of this "created an uncertain status regarding the implementation of the RAP." As of late 2021, I was unable to identify any follow-up action on the Pacific RAP, but civil society organizations have continued to call on the PIF leadership to implement UNSCR 1325 in the Pacific countries.

The de-prioritization of the WPS agenda has been apparent in other efforts by the PIF that missed the opportunity to deepen the engagement with issues of gender equality in peace and security. Most importantly, in September 2018 in Nauru, the PIF adopted the Boe Declaration of Regional Security (PIF 2018). Building on the Biketawa Declaration, the Boe Declaration reflects on multiple challenges faced by the Pacific Islands, explicitly expanding the concept of security to include issues of human, environmental, and cyber security (PIF 2018). While recognizing multiple inequalities and forms of structural discrimination, gender equality and the status of women are barely touched on. The Boe Declaration mentions UNSCR 1325 on one occasion, but there is no acknowledgment of the Pacific RAP whatsoever. The WPS agenda seems to have lost the momentum in the regional politics of the PIF, despite the promising early start in 2012.

National Implementation

While there is no evidence of a direct impact on gender equality in peace and security that could be attributed to the Pacific RAP, perhaps the most important outcome of this policy has been supporting an enabling environment for WPS implementation at national levels. Bhagwan-Rolls and Rolls (2019, 91) explicitly stated that the adoption of the RAP "has been recognized as a key regional mechanism to support the advancement of gender equality and women's rights in the Pacific region" as well as "in advocating for compliance with human rights standards such as CEDAW." Based on a series of regional consultations, the *Global Study on the Implementation of United Nations Security Council Resolution 1325* maintained that the Pacific RAP guided the development of a broader gender equality policy by Bougainville and a NAP by the Solomon Islands (Coomaraswamy 2015, 257). This NAP will be analyzed in more detail below, along with the NAPs adopted by Australia and New Zealand, the other members of the PIF.

The sociopolitical contexts of Australia and New Zealand on the one hand and the Solomon Islands on the other are vastly different. Yet the security politics and interests of these countries are interconnected, and this is reinforced by their membership in the PIF (George 2016). Australia and New Zealand play a distinct role in the PIF, both operating as donor countries. Neither experienced recent armed conflict on their territory and their engagement with the WPS agenda is predominantly focused on development, aid, and multilateral cooperation, including with the Solomon Islands. "The Australian National Action Plan on Women, Peace, and Security" (Government of Australia 2012), recently updated (Government of Australia 2021), and "New Zealand National Action Plan for the Implementation of United Nations Security Council Resolutions, Including 1325, on Women, Peace, and Security" (Government of New Zealand 2015) are ultimately outward-facing.

The Solomon Islands, by contrast, is a politically fragile post-conflict nation prone to protracted armed violence. Emerging from recent internal armed conflict (1998–2003), rooted in ethnic tensions between the Isatabu Freedom Movement and the Malaita Eagle Force, the Solomon Islands hosted between 2003 and 2017 the Regional Assistant Mission to Solomon Islands (RAMSI), led and funded primarily by Australia and New Zealand (see also Westendorf 2013). Internationally sponsored, the "Solomon Islands Women, Peace, and Security National Action Plan" (Government of the Solomon Islands 2017), again supported by Australia as well as UN Women and the United Nations Development Programme, is inward-looking and devoted to the gender impact of recent armed struggles.

Despite the significant geopolitical differences between the Solomon Islands and Australia and New Zealand, all grounded their NAPs in the human rights tradition, just as the Pacific RAP did. In linking gender equality to peace and security, Australia, New Zealand, and the Solomon Islands carefully avoided securitizing gender equality or essentializing women's roles, the risks common to the security and development paradigms of gender equality. Instead, Australia, New Zealand, and the Solomon Islands emphasized women's rights and participation, pointing to multiple forms of physical and structural inequalities that result from armed conflicts. The NAP of the Solomon Islands is perhaps most explicit in the engagement with the human rights paradigm of gender equality. It "recognises that women's experiences and priorities are essential to building inclusive security and sustainable peace grounded in human rights" (Government of the Solomon Islands 2017, 18). This NAP is founded on the premises of CEDAW and dedicates considerable attention to mapping the intersections between this major international women's rights bill and the WPS agenda. The NAPs of Australia and New Zealand also made references to CEDAW. Overall, they are relatively similar in how their respective policies envisaged gender equality. Both engaged with nuanced gender analysis of conflict and post-conflict situations, and how these situations affect diverse women. For instance, the NAP of New Zealand addressed the continuum between structural and physical violence in the following statement:

> Women's experiences of violence and discrimination in conflict societies tend to reflect the attitudes and social norms of the communities in which they live during times of peace. Violence and inequalities that women face in crises do not exist in a vacuum. Therefore, educating the whole communities and achieving core attitudinal and societal norm change is an important preventative measure. (Government of New Zealand 2015, 6)

This excerpt presents the gender awareness of multiple forms of discrimination and exclusions that lead to conflict-related violations of women's human rights. Similar awareness can be noted in the Australian NAP, which recognized gender equality as a cross-cutting issue across conflict and non-conflict, emphasizing the protection of human rights of women and girls in times of both peace and conflict (Government of Australia 2012, 7). The recently released second-generation NAP of Australia will also adopt "a human rights-based approach" as a principle guiding the implementation of the WPS agenda (Government of Australia 2021, 14–15). The sophisticated gender analysis around women's human rights and the emphasis on women's political empowerment and participation is ultimately evident in both cases of Australia and New Zealand.

The difference between the NAPs of Australia, New Zealand, and the Solomon Islands is more notable in the implementation strategy. All three NAPs designed an action matrix along with a monitoring and evaluation framework, including the key elements of impactful policy, identified by global research on NAPs, such as activities, roles and responsibilities, qualitative and quantitative indicators and timeframes, and sometimes also result statements or desirable outcomes (Coomaraswamy 2015, 241; Miller et al. 2014). But the strength and scope of these implementation frameworks varies. Of the three, the NAP of the Solomon Islands is the most specific, perhaps because it firmly embedded the WPS agenda in the local context. Australia and New Zealand ignored local challenges, including the situation of the Indigenous peoples or conflict-affected refugees living or seeking asylum in these countries (Dunn 2014; see also Lee-Koo and Trojanowska 2017; Shepherd 2016). This has made their policies more generic and abstract. The NAPs of New Zealand but especially Australia failed to translate the promising human rights discourse into concrete implementation steps and tangible impact (see also Lee-Koo 2014). There would be some effort to address this issue in the updated NAP of Australia released in 2021. The shortcomings of the generic WPS policy—and its paradoxical effects on the implementation practice—will be discussed in chapter 4, which is dedicated in full to Australia's engagement with the WPS agenda.

The PIF fosters geopolitical connectivity between its member states, including but not limited to the implementation of the WPS agenda. The Pacific RAP did not appear to produce a direct impact on gender equality across the Pacific Islands or to influence high-level political processes on peace and security, as evident in the lack of attention to UNSCR 1325 in the Boe Declaration. As such, the RAP has repeated some of the global challenges noted with regards to the human rights paradigm of gender equality, such as inadequate implementation and resistance of the key stakeholders to take action on the WPS agenda. The RAP has nonetheless supported the implementation of the WPS agenda by some of its member states and especially less-wealthy members such as the Solomon Island, as discussed above, but also by the Autonomous Region of Bougainville that adopted a broader "Policy for Women's Empowerment, Gender Equality, and Peace and Security" (Autonomous Bougainville Government 2016). It has done so by providing an enabling environment and through a policy commitment to gender equality in peace and security, and through mobilizing resources for WPS implementation from donor countries such as Australia and New Zealand.

CONCLUSION

This chapter explored the tensions in the global and regional interactions involved in the implementation of UNSCR 1325, centering the analysis around how gender equality has operated in the WPS policies of ASEAN and the PIF. The interrogation of these key regional organizations in Asia and the Pacific pointed to a conclusion that the regional experience with UNSCR 1325 has been somewhat different from the global WPS practice. While there is some evidence of RAPs and NAPs being mutually reinforcing, just like the *Global Study on the Implementation of United Nations Security Council Resolution 1325* (Coomaraswamy 2015) suggested, the traction of the WPS agenda has been more ambiguous in this region. I connected this ambiguity to the understanding of gender equality in relation to peace and security and the (dis)engagement with the paradigms identified at the global level. In particular, Asia and the Pacific refrained from the employment of the security paradigm of gender equality, which did not fit with preexisting security norms or conceptions of gender equality.

Securitized notions of gender equality that emphasized the obligation of international actors to protect women from sexual violence in conflict were rejected by both ASEAN and the PIF and their member states, who may have associated them with imperialist inclinations of global actors and powerful states, in the context of the colonial history of the region (Basu 2016a; 2016b; George 2014). After all, both Asia and the Pacific have a legacy of complex relationships with the UN system and developed certain skepticism toward UN frameworks that are sometimes perceived as evocative of foreign interference or even military interventions. The security paradigm that initially dominated the international WPS policy and practice may account for the delay in ASEAN's and the PIF's involvement with UNSCR 1325. Despite the development of other gender equality frameworks within these organizations and despite the relevance of the WPS agenda to the conflict-related challenges of Asia and the Pacific, specific action plans appeared in the region only in the second decade of UNSCR 1325.

Starting from 2010, however, Asia and the Pacific demonstrated—through regional organizations and their member states—an increasing interest in UNSCR 1325. A juxtaposition of the gender equality trajectory in ASEAN's and the PIF's implementation of the WPS agenda illustrated distinct ways in which the region meaningfully utilized global frameworks and connected them to local problems and understandings. But it also exposed how the WPS agenda can gain—and lose—momentum. The PIF released in 2012 the Pacific RAP, engaging with the human rights paradigm of gender equality and articulating a nuanced and robust approach to UNSCR 1325. Yet this important framework was subsequently followed by limited action and there has been little evidence of the implementation and impact of this policy on the PIF as a collective. The Pacific RAP has nonetheless supported the adoption of the NAP by the Solomon Islands and the development of WPS policy by Bougainville, and perhaps also applied additional pressure on Australia and New Zealand to release and update their NAPs.

ASEAN, by contrast, has recorded WPS-related developments only from 2017 onward. National efforts of some of ASEAN member states, in particular the Philippines and Indonesia, predated and influenced ASEAN's eventual commitment to the WPS agenda, with gender equality being approached through a development lens. UNSCR 1325 has evidently gained traction in ASEAN's politics more recently, yet the organization has continued to essentialize women's role in peacebuilding and to see gender equality as a means to development-driven ends. Moreover, a RAP has yet to be developed. It is hoped that the third decade of UNSCR 1325 could see a renewed commitment to the WPS agenda on the side of the PIF and the development of a RAP by ASEAN. Both would amplify the preexisting commitment to gender equality in peace and security and strengthen the implementation of relevant initiatives that have been underway in the region. They would also offer a remedy to gender inequalities and power imbalances that stem from multiple conflicts and emerging security challenges across Asia and the Pacific.

In sum, ASEAN and the PIF repeated some of the key dilemmas of gender equality policymaking, such as essentializing women's roles, typical for the development paradigm of gender equality, and inadequate implementation, prevalent in the human rights paradigm. These challenges have been situated within the context of the broader resistance of the region toward the security paradigm of gender equality. To this end, this chapter attempted to unravel problems that are common for gender equality policymaking processes but also reflect challenges that are unique to Asia and the Pacific and arise at the intersection of global and regional engagements. Chapters 3 and 4 will take this analysis of gender equality one step further and investigate how the goal of gender equality trickles down from the global promise of UNSCR 1325 to national implementation practice by government departments: first in the case study of the Philippines and then Australia.

NOTE

1. That is, the ten ASEAN dialogue partners (Australia, Canada, China, the European Union, India, Japan, New Zealand, the Republic of Korea, Russia, and the United States), other countries from Asia and the Pacific (Bangladesh, the Democratic People's Republic of Korea, Mongolia, Pakistan, Sri Lanka, and Timor-Leste), and one ASEAN observer (Papua New Guinea).

Chapter 3

Government of the Philippines

The Philippines pioneered a national-level policy on United Nations Security Council Resolution 1325 (UNSCR 1325) on Women, Peace, and Security (WPS) in the region of Asia and the Pacific (Barrow 2016; PeaceWomen 2021). Despite having been conflict-ridden for decades, the country has a strong history of institutionalization of women's rights through national policies and laws (Veneracion-Rallonza 2013). The WPS agenda fit into the preexisting sociolegal context to the point of eventually being integrated into human rights mechanisms (Trojanowska 2021). This resulted in the adoption of an approach to gender equality in the Philippine National Action Plans (NAPs) on WPS which has been driven by human rights principles and subsequently translated from policy to implementation practice.

The purpose of this chapter is to understand the implications and impact of the human rights paradigm of gender equality in the nested case study of the Philippines. As chapter 1 discussed in more detail, three distinct paradigms of gender equality emerged in operation with the global WPS agenda, focused on security, development, and human rights respectively. Each of the paradigms engaged in distinct ways with the objectives of women's *voices* and *experiences* in conflict prevention, conflict resolution, and post-conflict peacebuilding. *The security paradigm of gender equality* highlighted the protection of women from conflict-related sexual violence and the inclusion of women in the security sector, in particular in police and military roles. *The development paradigm of gender equality* was concerned with the empowerment of women in peacebuilding, yet often in gender-stereotyped roles as caretakers and peacemakers, and with the gender-differentiated needs of women in post-conflict relief and recovery. *The human rights paradigm of gender equality* advocated for women's participation in decision-making at all levels of peace and security governance and for women's protection from all forms of human rights violations and abuses. It appeared more promising than the other two paradigms as it was less prone to the co-optation of the goal of gender equality by more powerful agendas and other political priorities, be they security-driven effectiveness of international operations or economic development and growth.

Yet the empirical analysis of the Philippine implementation of UNSCR 1325 pointed to the conclusion that stabilizing the meaning of gender equality in line with the human rights paradigm may have both positive and negative effects. In the Philippines, this process has produced a significant impact on the work of government departments with preexisting commitments to gender equality, which could mitigate the gendered effects of armed conflicts without sacrificing the goal of gender equality. Simultaneously, the WPS agenda has had only limited influence on the National Security Policy and the upper echelons of the security sector where the human rights paradigm has proven incongruent with the dominant militaristic security discourse. In consequence, the human rights paradigm has reportedly improved the government's response to the impacts of armed conflicts on women's rights, but it did not go far enough to address the deepest root causes of these conflicts. This would be particularly evident for marginalized populations, such as Indigenous peoples of the Philippines and the Moros (i.e., Muslim minority) who have suffered from armed conflicts acutely, and yet the root causes of state-based violence against these groups have remained largely invisible in the WPS policy.

The empirical data for this chapter was gleaned from policy and institutional analysis of the WPS agenda in the Philippines, including the three Philippine National Action Plans on WPS adopted to date. A significant component of this data and analysis was drawn from field research in Manila, the Philippines in 2017 and interviews with over thirty policymakers and practitioners. Given the limited transparency of government processes in many conflict and post-conflict countries, I sought views from multiple stakeholders. The interviewees were mainly representatives from the current and former Philippine governments (including high-level agencies and large departments such as the Office of the Presidential Adviser on the Peace Process, the Philippine Commission on Women, the Department of National Defence, the Department of Social Welfare and Development, the Department of Interior and Local Governance, the Department of Foreign Affairs, the Commission on Human Rights, as well as the National Commission on Indigenous Peoples and the National Commission on Muslim Filipinos), local civil society organizations (including member organizations of the Philippine WPS network, Women Engaged in Action on 1325), and international partners (including UN agencies and international nongovernmental organizations operating in the Philippines).

Potential security risks to the interviewees discouraged posing sensitive questions at the time of my field research, which coincided with an unfolding security crisis related to increased terrorist activity in the second largest Island of the Philippines, Mindanao. The island was subsequently placed under martial law. Nonetheless, the interviews—in conjunction with policy and institutional analysis—provided crucial insights into how gender equality has been understood in the policy and practice of the WPS agenda in the Philippines, and what implications this has produced thus far.

This chapter starts with the historical background to armed conflicts and gender equality in the Philippines to contextualize the WPS agenda in the country-specific situation and policy environment. I then outline the elements of the human rights paradigm of gender equality and how the paradigm has been articulated and eventually institutionalized in the Philippine WPS policy and law. The effects of this institutionalization on the implementation practice are investigated subsequently as I delve into the notions of gender equality in government departments' engagement with the WPS agenda. In conclusion, I discuss the current and future implementation of the WPS agenda in the light of the post-2016 backlash on women's rights.

THE WOMEN, PEACE, AND SECURITY AGENDA AND ARMED CONFLICTS IN THE PHILIPPINES

The sociolegal context of the Philippines is characterized by the coexistence of protracted low-intensity armed conflicts with strong frameworks for gender equality, and women's rights in particular. This created a fertile ground for the WPS agenda. Not only did UNSCR 1325 prove highly pertinent to the complex situation of the Philippines, where women bear many of the consequence of armed violence (e.g., Barrow 2016), but it also resonated with prior gender-sensitive policies and laws. The relevance of the WPS agenda combined with the policy fit facilitated the diffusion of the agenda's objectives across the Philippine government, its projects, and programs. Below I discuss how this country-specific context shaped the approach to gender equality in peace and security.

Emerging from the complex history of colonialism (the country was occupied by Spain, the United Kingdom, the United States, and Japan), the Philippines has been conflict-ridden for decades (Veneracion-Rallonza 2013). Numerous intrastate conflicts and armed disputes have plagued the country at least since the 1960s. The major two relate to the government's fights with the Moro Islamic Liberation Front (MILF), struggling for self-determination of the Moro people in Mindanao, and with the Communist Party of the Philippines (CPP), striving to establish a communist society in the Philippines (Hall and Hoare 2015). Several smaller conflicts have been active as well, disproportionately affecting the Indigenous peoples of the Philippines.

Even though there have been some milestones in conflict resolution, such as the 2018 passing of the Bangsamoro Organic Law which was a crucial development in the peace process with the MILF, the situation is fragile (Barrow 2016, 9) and evolves dynamically. For instance, recent years saw the termination of peace talks with the CPP and the declaration of martial law in Mindanao due to increased terrorist threats on the island. The martial law was extended multiple times and only lifted in 2020. The conflicts in Philippines remain classified as low-intensity, but conflict-related death toll peaked in 2017 reaching the highest numbers in two decades (UCDP n.d.a), and the number of internally displaced people has grown rapidly (UNCHR 2019), especially in Mindanao, as a result of government-rebel fights. The current political situation of the Philippines is therefore described as a security crisis (Human Rights Watch 2019; 2020), which has been exacerbated by the COVID-19 pandemic (see Global Network of Women Peacebuilders 2021; Human Rights Watch 2021).

Despite the challenges of prolonged armed conflicts and armed violence, the Philippines has a strong history of women's rights movements advocacy and the institutionalization of gender equality. A national machinery for women's advancement in the form of the Philippine Commission on Women (PCW) (formerly known as the National Commission on the Role of the Filipino Women) was created in 1975. The Philippines was also one of the first countries worldwide to ratify the Convention on the Elimination of All Forms of Discrimination Against Women (CEDAW), in 1981 (Renshaw 2017). Since the early 1990s, gender-sensitive policies and laws have proliferated in the political landscape, including the Women in Development and Nation-Building Act, the Philippine Plan for Gender-Responsive Development, the Anti-Rape Act, the Rape Victim Assistance and Protection Act, the Anti-Trafficking in Persons Act, the Anti-Violence against Women and Their Children Act, and especially the Magna Carta of Women in the Philippines, which would lay the foundations for WPS implementation (for more, see Veneracion-Rallonza 2013).

Even though law enforcement remains an immense challenge in the Philippines (Human Rights Watch 2020), the country is commonly praised for the established policy and legal infrastructure that supports gender equality and has led to some positive outcomes. The World Economic Forum's Global Gender Gap Reports (WEF n.d.) until recently ranked the Philippines among the top ten countries, next to Scandinavian states and New Zealand, nearing the closure of the gender gap. The WEF's reports collect data on countries' gender equality performance, specifically the status of women relative to men, and the gaps across economic participation and opportunity, educational attainment, health and survival, and political empowerment. However, in 2020 and 2021, the Philippines dropped down significantly to the eighteenth and seventeenth places respectively (of over 150 countries included in the WEF report), presumably due to the impact of the evolving security crisis on the safety, livelihood, and political participation of women (WEF 2020; 2021).

Given the established gender equality infrastructure and the history of conflict, it was unsurprising when the Philippines became the first country in the entire region of Asia and the Pacific to develop a national WPS policy (Barrow 2016). The administration of President Gloria Macapagal Arroyo launched in 2010 "The Philippine National Action Plan on UNSCR 1325 and 1820" (Government of the Philippines 2010) after broad consultations with civil society across the Philippine islands, including Mindanao (Veneracion-Rallonza 2013). The first NAP was followed by two further iterations. The administration of President Benigno Aquino III reviewed and revised the 2010 NAP, turning it in 2014 into a second-generation plan under the same title (Government of the Philippines 2014). After the completion of the NAP in 2016, the third iteration of the "National Action Plan on Women, Peace, and Security" (Government of the Philippines 2017) was launched in 2017 under the presidency of Rodrigo Duterte and its implementation has been underway. Ultimately, the Philippine WPS policy has been in place for over a decade and has operated under three radically different government administrations. And yet the approach to gender equality would be rather consistent, resonating with earlier national frameworks on women's human rights.

NATIONAL ACTION PLANS ON WOMEN, PEACE, AND SECURITY

With three NAPs released to date, the Philippines has established a strong WPS track record. Globally, NAPs have become a major vehicle for the diffusion of the WPS agenda beyond the UN system and a tool to translate global promises into national accountability (True 2016; Swaine 2009; Tryggestad 2014). Put simply, NAPs provide the blueprint for the WPS policy of a given country, whether domestic or foreign (see also Miller et al. 2014, 10), and offer a mechanism for national implementation of the gender equality goal in peace and security (see also chapter 2). NAPs are typically two-part documents consisting of a narrative report that outlines the country-specific context and challenges pertaining to UNSCR 1325, and an implementation framework that lays out activities, roles, and monitoring and evaluation indicators. This is important to note because a relatively coherent approach to gender equality embedded in human rights principles has guided the three Philippine NAPs across the narrative part and the implementation framework. Moreover, the Philippines would adopt the human rights paradigm consistently across the three iterations.

From the outset, the Philippine NAPs firmly founded the gender equality discourse on human rights principles, situating this discourse within the country-specific context and history. Developed in a process of consultation with civil society and conflict-affected groups (Veneracion-Rallonza 2013), the narrative report of the 2010 NAP presented a brief, albeit pertinent, analysis of ongoing conflicts and their impacts, pointing out the root causes of armed violence across the Philippine islands. These included: uneven access to resources, political rivalry among powerful dynasties, warlordism, proliferation of small arms and light weapons, poverty, poor governance, and finally discrimination and marginalization of minority groups such as Indigenous peoples across the country, the Moro people in Mindanao, and women more broadly (Government of the Philippines 2010, 3–5). By the same token, the NAP acknowledged some of the gendered causes and effects of armed conflicts, grounding the WPS policy into the specific challenges faced by the Philippines. It was in this sociopolitical context of armed conflicts and prolonged insecurity and violence that the rights and participation of women were placed at the center stage of the Philippine WPS policy. The first NAP set the goals for the implementation of the WPS agenda as follows:

> To ensure the protection of women's rights in situations of armed conflict and prevention of violation of their rights during and after armed conflict; empower women and ensure their active and meaningful participation in peace building process; and promote and mainstream a gender perspective in all aspects of peace building, including conflict prevention and resolution. (Government of the Philippines 2010, 78)

The NAP rested on two "substantive pillars" of protection and participation as well as two "support pillars" of gender mainstreaming and monitoring and evaluation that served to enhance the implementation of the WPS agenda (Government of the Philippines 2010, 22). Even though protection remained the central theme throughout the 2010 NAP, a spectrum of human rights violations and abuses was considered within this WPS policy beyond narrowly defined conflict-related sexual violence.

The human rights paradigm would become more explicit and sophisticated in the Philippine WPS policy over the years. While the 2014 NAP made no modifications to the narrative report from 2010, the 2017 NAP engaged with human rights principles more directly. It sought "to embed the language of women's human rights, specifically gender equality, as provided for in the Convention on the Elimination of All Forms of Discrimination Against Women" (Government of the Philippines 2017, 12). Moreover, women's participation would be prioritized over the protection of women's rights. "Privileging of women's agency" was justified in the NAP in terms of lessons learned from long-standing implementation of the WPS agenda in the Philippines (Government of the Philippines 2017, 14). A government representative explained that "protection doesn't necessarily lead to empowerment; women have to participate first, women have to be empowered and have voice so that they can promote their rights" (OPAPP 1, interview). In addition to the growing emphasis on women's participation, this excerpt showcased the gradual sophistication of the WPS discourse and the recognition of the mutually reinforcing nature of participation and protection in the realization of the objectives of the WPS agenda. In all of this, the NAP's discourse on gender equality clearly located the WPS agenda within the field of human rights.

The human rights paradigm of gender equality was not limited to the narrative report of the Philippine NAPs but extended onto the implementation framework. This is important to note because "the effective translation of the resolution [1325] into transformative policy and practice remains the greatest challenge" (Swaine 2009, 421), and this problem will be evident in chapter 4 in the Australian case study. Many NAPs adopted worldwide put forward a relatively nuanced narrative report only to follow with a simplistic action matrix that fails to facilitate effective implementation (Coomaraswamy 2015; Miller et al. 2014; Trojanowska et al. 2018). By contrast, the Philippine NAPs—at least the first two iterations—were designed as result-oriented documents where high-level objectives were linked to implementation measures.

The 2010 NAP defined desired outcomes alongside action points, roles, and responsibilities of government departments, and monitoring and evaluation indicators that were relatively specific, time-bound, and relevant. In doing so, the 2010 NAP aligned with the principles of global good practice recommended by the UN Secretary-General (S/2010/173, para. 7). The 2014 NAP refined the earlier matrix making it more concise and systematic. Improvements included the reduction of the number of action points and the growing specification of indicators. Barrow (2016, 26–27) suggested that the predominantly descriptive and quantitative indicators in the Philippine NAPs may not be sufficient to comprehensively assess whether implementation is effective. But the framework of both the 2010 and 2014 NAP was comparatively strong, constituting, in the words of a government representative, "an outcome-based instrument" to implement the WPS agenda in the Philippine country-specific context and policy environment (OPAPP 2, interview).

The revision and growing specification of the NAP implementation framework was not the only milestone observed in 2014 or even the most important one. In that year, the Philippine government issued a dedicated policy to integrate the WPS agenda into earlier human rights mechanisms, the 2009 Magna Carta of Women. Described as "a comprehensive women's human rights law," the Magna Carta of Women is a law and a national mechanism for the compliance with CEDAW (PCW n.d.). In addition to generic gender equality provisions, the Magna Carta of Women stipulated provisions pertaining to the role and protection of women affected by conflicts, providing the conceptual foundations for the first Philippine NAP, which was adopted merely a year later.

In 2014, the NAP was placed under the jurisdiction of the Magna Carta for Women with the adoption of the Joint Memorandum Circular No. 2014-01 on "Integration of Women, Peace, and Security Programs, Activities, and Projects (PAPs) in Annual Gender and Development (GAD) Plans and Budgets (GPBs) and Gender and Development Accomplishments Reports (GAD ARs)" (JMC No. 2014-01). The JMC No. 2014-01 extended the budgeting and reporting requirement of the Magna Carta of Women onto WPS, formally aligning the NAPs with preexisting women's human rights instruments. According to government interviewees, this was a pivotal step in the implementation of the WPS agenda, one that ingrained the NAPs into the policy and legal environment of the Philippines to ensure a long-term and sustained commitment (OPAPP 1, interview; OPAPP 2, interview). Research praised this development, maintaining that the Philippine NAPs demonstrated "innovation in advancing broader goals of gender equality and women's empowerment" (Amling et al. 2016, 25). Moreover, through these bureaucratic and legal processes, the JMC No. 2014-01 cemented the understanding of gender equality as a women's human rights issue.

The importance of the national institutionalization of the WPS agenda through the JMC No. 2014-01 would become evident in the aftermath of the 2016 election of President Rodrigo Duterte and the backlash against women's rights. The presidency of Duterte was characterized by "misogyny and machismo" in the words of a civil society interviewee (CSO 3, interview) and "bravado" in the words of a UN representative (UN 1, interview). Duterte's national leadership feeds on hypermasculinity and his repeated sexist "rape jokes" sparked public outrage in the Philippines and internationally (Tanyag 2018). Evidently, the post-2016 political environment has been far from supportive to gender equality. The 2017 NAP launched by Duterte's administration, while rhetorically strong and embedded in the human rights discourse as noted above, turned out more tokenistic than the previous iterations. The NAP still outlined goals and objectives, but instead of a standard implementation matrix, it did so in a less effective narrative form with no division of roles or responsibilities between government departments. Hence, the overall accountability of the government to the WPS agenda has diminished in the 2017 iteration, which has supposedly left the government departments with greater freedom in choosing which objectives they intend to act on. Some of my interviewees from civil society and international organizations perceived this major weakness of the 2017 NAP as symptomatic of the increasingly constraining environment to the WPS agenda since President Duterte assumed power in 2016. One of them stated with concern that "it's going to be tough to ensure the [2017] NAP will be implemented" (UN 1, interview). Nevertheless, the accountability mechanism established in 2014 with the integration of the NAPs under the Magna Carta of Women has secured the ongoing implementation of the WPS agenda, as will be discussed in the following.

GOVERNMENT'S IMPLEMENTATION OF THE NATIONAL ACTION PLANS

The Philippine NAPs are set as a whole-of-government policy, in line with the Presidential Executive Order 865, with which the first NAP was adopted back in 2010 (President of the Philippines 2010). Large departments responsible for service delivery, security, and justice have been envisaged as the major stakeholders in the Philippine WPS policy, with their work overseen by two high-level policymaking agencies located in the Office of the President: the Office of the Presidential Adviser on the Peace Process and the Philippine Commission on Women. Despite philosophical and operational differences between government departments and agencies accountable to the NAPs with their vastly different functions, the understanding of gender equality has proven relatively similar. It resonated with human rights principles in line with the JMC No. 2014-01. Yet the impact of this fixed meaning and purpose of gender equality in the WPS agenda has varied, depending on preexisting priorities and organizational cultures identified in the departments. More specifically, departments working with service delivery have reported significant progress in implementing the NAPs as the human rights paradigm has fit into the preexisting work on gender equality, deepening the gender analysis of conflict situations. Conversely, the impact on the security sector, while still noticeable, has been more superficial due to the incongruence of human rights principles with the preexisting militaristic security discourse. The justice branch of the government presented yet another case because the contentious politics prevented meaningful engagement with the WPS agenda, at the time of my field research.

The rest of this chapter will trace the trajectory and operation of gender equality in the implementation practice of government departments with a view to understand the implications and impact of these processes. My analysis relies heavily on the pronouncements of government representatives and other stakeholders, as well as on civil society reports on UNSCR 1325 (where available). This is in recognition of scholarly literature on WPS that is still emerging.

The Impact on Peace and Security Policymaking in the Philippines

The Philippine WPS policy has been articulated by the Office of the Presidential Adviser on the Peace Process (OPAPP) and the Philippine Commission on Women (PCW), both being high-level policymaking agencies. Neither has the responsibility for the implementation of the NAPs as such, but jointly OPAPP and PCW provide policy direction with regards to the WPS agenda in the Philippines. These agencies chair the high-level National Steering Committee on Women, Peace, and Security and the lower-level Technical Working Group on Women, Peace, and Security that coordinate the whole-of-government effort in implementing the NAPs. Furthermore, OPAPP and PCW led the development of the JMC No. 2014-01, in which they collectively framed gender equality as a human rights issue falling under the mandate of the Magna Carta of Women. This framing influenced high-level policymaking processes with regards both to the protection of women's rights in the situation of conflict and insecurity and to the participation of women in peace and security governance.

During separate interviews with OPAPP and PCW, I found out that the WPS agenda filled an important gap in the work of both agencies. Specifically, the NAPs connected data on armed conflicts in the Philippines with evidence on the status of women across the country. In their high-level advisory role, OPAPP collects from other departments data on active armed conflicts and ongoing peace processes to advise the president, whereas PCW gleans similar data on the situation of women. Representatives from PCW admitted that until the NAP adoption in 2010, little had been done to cross-analyze the data from both agencies that would ultimately capture the situation of conflict-affected women in the Philippines (PCW 1-2, interview). The NAPs laid out a framework to monitor human rights violations committed against women in conflict and post-conflict settings. OPAPP and PCW reportedly utilized this new knowledge to advise the president and government departments on appropriate protection measures (see also Government of the Philippines 2010, 9).

Equally importantly, the WPS agenda contributed to the high-level advocacy by OPAPP and PCW for the increased participation of women in peace and security governance. The appointment of Miriam Coronel-Ferrer as the chairperson of the peace panel between the government and the MILF, with her subsequently becoming the first woman in the world to sign a major peace accord (i.e., the 2014 Comprehensive Agreement on the Bangsamoro), was one of the outcomes of this advocacy (Nobel Women's Initiative 2014; see also Coomaraswamy 2015). Some positive, albeit slower, impact of the NAPs was also noted in local governance as recorded by civil society reports that monitored the representation of women in relevant government bodies, between 2010 and 2014 (see Nario-Galace and Piscano 2010; 2011; Piscano et al. 2012; Natividad et al. 2013; Veneracion-Rallonza and Rallonza 2014). Sadly, the "Women Count" initiative of the Global Network of Women Peacebuilders concluded in 2014.

While OPAPP and PCW have engaged in high-level advisory and capacity building of government departments in the implementation of the WPS agenda, it is essentially the role of those other departments to operationalize the NAP objectives through specific projects and programs. The JMC No. 2014-01 provided OPAPP and PCW with a mechanism to monitor government funds dedicated to the NAPs and, in this context, to ensure that departments allocate and report on relevant spending. But OPAPP and PCW exert less control over the specific work of the departments, with the representative from PCW stating that the agency had "no teeth" to enforce WPS implementation in ways other than monitoring and reporting the progress (PCW 2, interview; see also Amling et al. 2016, 35). This remained in the power of individual departments that implement the NAPs through projects and programs.

The Impact on the Delivery of Essential Services to Conflict-Affected Women

The Department of Social Welfare and Development (DSWD), the Department of Interior and Local Governance (DILG), and the Department of Foreign Affairs (DFA) are large government departments that deliver essential services to the Philippine population, including conflict-affected women, whether at home or, as in the case of DFA, overseas. These departments had a preexisting engagement with issues of gender equality prior to the NAPs, most commonly with the issue of violence against women and the needs of women in conflict and post-conflict situations. Various levels of impact of the WPS agenda could be noted in the policy and practice of DSWD, DILG, and DFA that have overlapping, albeit different, mandates. While their approach was not always distinctive from their previous work on gender equality, all of them appeared better equipped to respond to the impacts of conflicts and to mitigate more effectively their effects on women. Over time the engagement with the human rights paradigm became more explicit as a result of JMC No. 2014-01.

To start with, DSWD maps the needs of the entire Philippine population, typically socioeconomic or sometimes health related, including the needs of women. In regions affected by conflicts, the department operates in close collaboration with agencies responsible for government-sponsored relief and recovery program, called "Peaceful and Resilient Communities" (PAyapa at MAsaganang PamayaNAn, or PAMANA for short). At the outset, the implementation of the WPS agenda centered around women's recovery needs in conflict and post-conflict situations, as this aligned most strongly with the department's preexisting work and the understanding of gender equality as a developmental issue. During a group interview with DSWD and PAMANA officers, I learned that the department's engagement with the NAPs was concrete, tangible, and highly practical. While not bringing an entirely new agenda to DSWD's long-standing gender equality efforts, the NAPs strengthened the conflict lens and, in doing so, improved the overall responsiveness of the department to humanitarian crises, with a view to upholding women's rights and fulfilling women's needs. The departmental-level action plan on WPS showcased during the interview comprised of specific action points, focused on gender-sensitive assistance. After the Marawi crisis broke out following government-rebel fights in Mindanao and the declaration of martial law in May 2017, an important aspect of DSWD's work under the NAP was, for example, to have safety protocols in place to ensure that recovery packages for female evacuees contained essential products, such as sanitary napkins and pants, as well as a safety whistle to protect women from violence in evacuation centers.

Over time, women's participation in peacebuilding would also be highlighted. In the implementation of the third NAP, the focus shifted subtly from women's needs to their participation and empowerment. Support to decision-making capacity of local women was placed at the forefront of projects undertaken under the 2017 NAP, with the interviewees emphasizing that "more weight is now on women's participation and women's involvement in peace processes and peacebuilding" (PAMANA 1-2, interview). The PAMANA officers explained that this decision has been motivated by the acknowledgment of slower progress in that area of the WPS agenda. That is, DSWD reportedly made headway throughout the course of the 2010 and 2014 NAPs in developing departmental capacity to provide gender-sensitive assistance to conflict-affected women, in particular through the "Women in Especially Difficult Circumstances Program" (for more, see OPAPP 2016b, 63–64). Women's participation in peacebuilding, by contrast, did not improve nearly as much, and therefore it became a priority for DSWD in the implementation of the 2017 NAP. All in all, DSWD made concerted efforts to operationalize the gender equality objective of the NAPs and translate high-level priorities into concrete projects that benefit conflict-affected women, and importantly, the incentive for the participation of women was not instrumentalized or utilized for other goals.

DILG, a department that oversees the engagement of the Philippine government with local governments in order to strengthen their capacity to deliver services to their local constituencies, appeared to have been less exposed to WPS as a distinct agenda. In a group interview, representatives from DILG reported on several projects conducted by the department targeting gender equality, women's rights and violence against women, including in conflict-affected regions. With the exception of one participant, the interviewees had a rather limited understanding of UNSCR 1325, essentially drawing no distinction between the WPS agenda and other gender-related work undertaken by the department. The report published by OPAPP (2016b) similarly found that a major challenge for DILG was the lack of conflict-disaggregated data and this may explain the difficulty that the interviewees exhibited in pointing to specific projects with a primary focus on the WPS agenda. Nonetheless, DILG was at that time reportedly developing an internal policy prescribing the engagement with local governments with regards to the 2017 NAP (DILG 4, interview). However, at the time of the interview, the representatives were unable to elaborate, explaining that concrete initiatives on WPS were typically identified at local levels (DILG 1-2-3, interview).

While the local implementation of UNSCR 1325 is beyond the scope of this chapter, I was further informed that the progress across the country varied significantly, depending on the knowledge and political priorities of local leaders. Some local governments have been directly involved in the NAP implementation even to the point of localization of the WPS agenda and developing dedicated Local Action Plans on WPS. Others, however, had no awareness of UNSCR 1325 (LGU, interview; CSO 6, interview; see also WE Act 1325 and GNWP 2017).

DFA was another department involved in the Philippine NAPs that provided services to conflict-affected populations, albeit in the context of overseas employment of Filipinos in neighboring and other countries. Even though the NAPs were domestically focused by design—that is, the WPS agenda was primarily applied to the country-specific context in the Philippines as opposed to international engagements, foreign policy, or UN peacekeeping operations (for more on inward- and outward-focused NAPs, see Miller et al. 2014)—DFA was proactive in WPS implementation. During an interview, a representative from DFA presented a strong case for the department's involvement under the NAPs due to the commonplace conflict-related trauma among Filipinos in foreign employment. According to the interviewee, the majority of foreign employees experienced conflict-related hardships which influenced their decision to flee the country. An estimate of 10 percent of

Filipinos, or 8 million people, were overseas workers (Commission on the Filipinos Overseas n.d.), and DFA had a responsibility to provide protection and assistance to them. Women were largely overrepresented in this cohort. DFA integrated the WPS agenda into predeployment training for government officials and further in the psychosocial assistance services available to the Filipinos employed overseas, in recognition of the long-term impact of conflict trauma (DFA, interview).

The major responsibility of DFA in the implementation of the WPS agenda, however, is related to guiding the Philippine engagement on UNSCR 1325 with partner governments and international organizations, especially the UN (see also OPAPP 2016b). For example, DFA typically oversaw and provided inputs for statements delivered by the Philippines at the UN Security Council's open debates on WPS, which were often used to report on the participation of women in formal and informal peace processes and peace negotiations in the Philippines as well as on the support to women's resilience and community leadership (e.g., S/PV.8382). At the time of the interview however, the issue of foreign engagement was highly contentious, with President Duterte repeatedly rejecting foreign funds in offensive public statements (e.g., *CNN Philippines* 2017). This function of DFA in the implementation of the NAPs was not brought up by the interviewee during the two meetings I had with the department, presumably due to its political sensitivity.

The role of government departments and supporting agencies that provide essential services to conflict-affected women—whether DSWD and PAMANA agencies, DILG and local governments, or DFA—is a critical component of the implementation of the WPS agenda in the Philippines. It also is paramount to the realization of the agenda's objectives, including the goal of gender equality. These departments are uniquely positioned to translate high-level objectives into tangible outcomes, and in this role, they were supported by local civil society organizations and international partners whose work lies outside the scope of this chapter. Collectively, these actors made significant progress in WPS implementation, reported during the interviews with government representatives and detailed in the government's progress report on WPS (OPAPP 2016).

DSWD, DILG, and DFA rarely had the capacity to address the root causes of the ongoing conflicts and instead attempted to mitigate their effects in a gender- and conflict-sensitive manner, whether through relief and recovery assistance or through concrete support to women's participation in local governance. The WPS agenda connected with the preexisting commitments to gender equality identified in these departments, enhancing their capability and responsiveness to conflict-affected women and sharpening the focus on women's rights and needs. Even though UNSCR 1325 was not always perceived to be a distinct agenda and some actors lacked expert knowledge on

WPS, the NAPs supported a greater focus on the participation and well-being of conflict-affected women. The traction of the WPS agenda would be different in the departments with more limited exposure to human rights principles prior to the NAPs, particularly in the security sector.

The Impact on the Security Sector and Protection of Conflict-Affected Women

The security sector plays a distinct role in the implementation of the WPS agenda in conflict-ridden Philippines. The Department of National Defence (DND) and two executive agencies, the Armed Forces of the Philippines (AFP) and the Philippine National Police (PNP), have been accountable to the NAPs. Due to their "significant role in protecting the physical safety and security of women and girls from gender-based violence and in identifying their specific needs in the times of crisis," the AFP and the PNP in particular were envisaged as "frontline enforcement agencies" of the NAP (Government of the Philippines 2010, 6). Just like in other government departments, an overarching approach of the Philippine security sector would align the implementation of the WPS agenda with the human rights paradigm of gender equality, yet with a strong emphasis on the protection of women from human rights violations and abuses in conflict environments. The NAPs have reportedly strengthened the capability of the security sector to respond to diversified communities precisely through the improved protection of conflict-affected women, many of whom belong to marginalized groups. But while this enhanced protection effort by all means constitutes a positive change as a result of the NAPs, the WPS agenda has yet to influence the upper echelons of the security sector, which continue to lack gender awareness across the board. The impact of the WPS agenda on the security sector in the Philippines was therefore assessed as crucial yet fragmented or, in the words of a research participant, "not leveled" (AFP, interview).

State-based violence is rife in the Philippines, which has been plagued by multiple intrastate conflicts (see UCDP n.d.a). Contextually, the WPS agenda was approached by the security sector through a protection lens and with a focus on the rights and needs of women in conflict areas (see WE Act 1325 and GNWP 2017). As early as in 2012, local civil society organizations, often in collaboration with OPAPP and PCW, began conducting capacity-building activities for the AFP and the PNP on the WPS agenda to sensitize the agencies to the gender-differentiated impacts of conflicts (WE Act 1325 and GNWP 2017, 78–96). UNSCR 1325's objectives were subsequently integrated into compulsory modules for the military and the police forces deployed to challenging conflict and disaster environments. The representatives from the AFP, the PNP, and the DND affirmed the importance of the inclusion of the WPS agenda in these modules and attributed the increased gender awareness among their personnel precisely to the NAPs. A DND interviewee highlighted that the department on the whole was "more sensitive now, more conscious about how we are managing women in disaster and in conflict settings" (DND 1, interview), and this account was supported by the AFP and the PNP in separate interviews.

Interestingly, the WPS agenda impacted the security sector not only through strengthening a gender lens but also through increasing cultural sensitivity toward conflict-affected groups (DND 1-2-3, interview; AFP, interview). The overwhelming majority of conflict-affected women in the Philippines are Indigenous and Moro women. Cases of abuses, including sexual and gender-based violence, against these women by the military and the police have been reported across the country, and the relationship of Indigenous peoples or the Moros with state security forces has been typically characterized by distrust. This very aspect was capitalized on by the National Commission on Indigenous Peoples (NCIP) and the National Commission on Muslim Filipinos (NCMF), which promote the rights and interests of their minority groups in the predominantly Roman Catholic Philippines.

While their roles within the Philippine Government are relatively similar, the mandate of the NCMF is more complicated than that of NCIP due to the fact that the Bangsamoro Autonomous Region in Muslim Mindanao, where the Muslim population constitutes the majority, remains the only autonomous region in the Philippines. Similar to the NCIP, the NCMF works toward improving the status of the Muslim minority across the country, yet as part of the Philippine Government, the NCMF is at the same time expected not to step into the politicized mandate of the government of the Bangsamoro Autonomous Region in Muslim Mindanao (NCMF, interview), where the conflict is ongoing. However, both commissions have been involved in the Philippine NAPs since the early days and have been active members of the National Steering Committee on Women, Peace, and Security, utilizing the WPS agenda to educate other departments on issues of the safety and rights of marginalized women.

Because of the NAPs, the security sector was reportedly able to build a better relationship with conflict-affected communities. My interviewees, whether from the security agencies or from the commissions, admitted that local WPS meetings of the AFP and the PNP with conflict-affected groups were, in some instances, the first time these actors gathered in one room (NCIP, interview; AFP, interview). Furthermore, at the time of my field research, President Duterte made outrageous public "rape jokes" suggesting that his soldiers would not be held accountable for sexual abuses against female rebels in Mindanao committed during martial law (see *Guardian* 2017). And yet my interviewee stated that "the AFP didn't buy it" (OPAPP 3, interview) and "nobody laughed" at this "joke" of the commander-in-chief

(PNP 1, interview). Both interviewees explained that thanks to the WPS agenda and the NAPs, AFP and PNP officers were trained on and aware of human rights of women in conflict and the potential consequences of breaching them. But while this impact of the NAPs on the consciousness of the AFP and the PNP was powerful, sadly, it did not translate into the upper echelons of the security sector.

Despite the growing gender and cultural sensitiveness of the AFP and the PNP, further analysis of the security sector in the Philippines suggests that its masculinist identity remained largely unchanged. The focus on gender inequalities within the security sector was more limited in the context of the NAPs. DND introduced gender-sensitive policies over the past decades, including gender quotas (e.g., WE Act 1325 and GNWP 2017), yet these developments appeared to be only weakly related to the WPS agenda. Amling and colleagues (2016) argued that the NAPs provided an additional incentive for increasing the participation of women in the security sector; however, the bulk of scholarly literature on the Philippine military failed to mention the WPS agenda on any occasion (e.g., Hall 2012; 2016). This points to the conclusion that the WPS agenda had little impact on the organizational culture of the security institutions.

This conclusion could be further drawn from some of the candid interviews. When asked explicitly whether women's participation in the military was affected by the NAPs or rather by preexisting policies, a DND interviewee replied by saying, "That's a good question," adding after reflection that the WPS agenda has strengthened the institutionalization of these earlier frameworks. Representatives from the PNP were even more hesitant toward attributing any such impact to UNSCR 1325 and complained that the NAPs were heavily focused on the protection of the rights of women in conflict regions, but they did little to challenge the gender biases within the agency itself. The interviewees explicitly stated that the security institutions "perpetuate gender inequalities" (PNP 1, interview). When it came to professional promotion and deployment to risky environments in the Philippines or to UN peace operations, male favoritism reportedly prevails, and the WPS agenda did not reform the security institutions on the inside (PNP 1-2, interview).

Even more disappointing was the fact that the gender equality goal of the NAPs has not influenced the overall security policy of the Philippines to any significant extent. The prime policy document that stipulates the Philippine domestic, foreign, and military affairs is the National Security Policy. Neither the 2011–2016 policy launched by President Benigno Aquino III nor the one endorsed by President Rodrigo Duterte for 2017–2022 bore any marks of engagement, whether explicit or implicit, with UNSCR 1325 or the NAPs. Both policies involved scattered references to violence against women but without making sense of the impact of these issues on large political processes related to national security. Evidently, gender equality was not perceived as an issue having security connotations, presumably due to the incongruence of the human rights paradigm that dominated the NAPs with the security discourse that was increasingly militarized and masculinized under the national leadership of President Duterte. Ultimately, the security sector appeared to have lacked the knowledge of gender equality as a complex security issue.

The Impact on Justice and the Rule of Law

The branch of justice was even less marked by the impact of the WPS agenda. As previously discussed, high levels of state-based violence, including human rights abuses of conflict-affected women, commonly occur across the Philippines. Respect for the rule of law and fighting the widespread impunity are prerequisites to building an equal and just society in the Philippines and clearly fall under the remit of the WPS agenda. The Department of Justice (DOJ) and the Commission on Human Rights (CHR) were therefore envisioned among the crucial actors in WPS implementation in the Philippines, with DOJ having been among the founding members of the National Steering Committee on Women, Peace, and Security in the early years of the NAP. At the time of my field research, however, DOJ appeared to have no involvement in the NAPs, whereas the operation of CHR was threatened amid contentions politics.

In 2017, DOJ had no WPS focal point I could reach with a request for an interview. Despite attempts, I was unable to identify representatives who had recently engaged with WPS implementation on behalf of DOJ. By working backward and with fragmented information, I was nonetheless able to establish that the former secretary of DOJ, Leila de Lima, played a significant role in the drafting of the first Philippine NAP back in 2010 (Veneracion-Rallonza 2014, 2). Yet she was imprisoned between 2017 and 2020, allegedly for corruption, although Lima called herself "Duterte's first political prisoner" (Goetz 2017). Formerly chair of the CHR, Leila de Lima investigated the violence of Duterte's regime as the mayor of Davao City in Mindanao. Later in her function as a senator, she also condemned extrajudicial killings in Duterte's "War on Drugs" (Goetz 2017). It appeared that since her leaving DOJ in 2015, little engagement of the department with the NAPs could be tracked. This conclusion was confirmed by the civil society actors whom I interviewed for my research and who complained about DOJ's limited involvement in the NAPs (CSO 4, interview). It was also corroborated by the NAPs report published by OPAPP (2016b) where references to any initiatives undertaken by the DOJ were minimal.

By contrast, the CHR had an ongoing involvement with the WPS agenda, but the operation of the commission was threatened in the post-2016 political environment. As a quasi-government agency, the CHR is mandated to guard the Philippines' compliance with International Human Rights Law, with International Humanitarian Law, and—with respect to gender equality—with CEDAW and the Magna Carta of Women. Pursuant to the latter, the CHR was appointed as the gender ombudsman in the Philippines. The NAPs—which the commission has continued to support—added a conflict lens onto its work on gender equality (CHR, interview). Accordingly, the CHR engaged in capacity trainings for government departments and agencies working on the NAP, focusing on the protection of civil and political rights of conflict-affected populations (CHR, interview). Of particular importance for the CHR was the work with the AFP and the PNP, again due to the state-based violence in conflict regions. However, President Duterte has repeatedly called for the abolition of the commission since taking power in 2016. Negative attitudes from the current government toward the CHR were clear at the time of the interview, and shortly after my field research, the CHR's budget was slashed, leaving the agency with an uncertain future. While the commission continues its important work, it does so in a constraining political environment.

CONCLUSION

The Philippine WPS policy has a strong history of institutionalization, falling under the umbrella of the government's obligations to human rights instruments, including CEDAW. UNSCR 1325 resonated with the preexisting gender equality infrastructure, and the NAPs have been driven by the human rights paradigm. Developed in a collaborative process with significant inputs from civil society, as well as support from international partners, the Philippine NAPs are envisioned as a vehicle to increase women's participation and leadership in peace and security processes and to better protect and respond to violations of human rights against conflict-affected women, thereby producing tangible impact on the lives of these women. Significant progress in implementing the WPS agenda at the national level has followed, with the Philippines remaining the regional leader in Asia and the Pacific and perhaps also one of the global leaders. For example, the *Global Study on the Implementation of United Nations Security Council Resolution 1325* featured the Philippines as a good practice example of women's participation and leadership in the peace process of the government with MILF, which resulted in the inclusion of gender-sensitive provisions in the 2014 Comprehensive Agreement on the Bangsamoro (Coomaraswamy 2015, 43). This example shows the real-life impact of WPS advocacy on gender equality opportunities and outcomes.

What is quite unique in the Philippine case study is the translation of the WPS agenda from the NAPs into binding national jurisdiction (see also

Trojanowska 2021). Under the leadership of the Office of the Presidential Adviser on the Peace Process and the Philippine Commission on Women, the NAPs have been placed under the human rights mandate of the Magna Carta of Women since 2014. Not only has this secured the ongoing implementation of the WPS agenda by the Philippine Government and strengthened the national accountability to UNSCR 1325 (see also Amling et al. 2016), but it has also cemented the human rights paradigm of gender equality. Despite the unfavorable political climate post-2016 that has accompanied the populist-nationalist regime of President Duterte, the institutional structure built around the NAPs has enabled continued WPS implementation in the Philippines even in the backdrop of evident backlash against women's rights.

However, in this chapter I have also identified some paradoxical consequences in the work of the government departments, which have followed the stabilizing of the meaning of gender equality in the WPS agenda in line with the human rights paradigm. In the departments with preexisting commitments to gender equality, in particular the Department of Social Welfare and Development, the Department of Interior and Local Governance, and the Department of Foreign Affairs, the NAPs have reportedly led to crucial improvements of service delivery to conflict-affected women. This is despite the fact that the WPS agenda was not always recognized as a distinct policy and despite the lack of conflict-disaggregated data in some departments. The interviewed representatives were unanimous in emphasizing that because of the NAPs they were better equipped to assist women in conflict and post-conflict situations.

While the fixed meaning of gender equality has clearly prevented the co-optation of the objective for security-driven ends, it has also resulted in virtually no impact of the WPS agenda on certain segments of the Philippine government. The state security institutions, such as the Department of National Defence, the Armed Forces of the Philippines, and the Philippine National Police, have enhanced their protection efforts and improved their respective relationships with conflict-affected minority groups, but their masculinist identity has not been reformed. Similarly, the National Security Policy of the Philippines has remained untouched by UNSCR 1325. I argued that this was due to the persistent conceptual separation between the human rights and security issues in the Philippines. Perceived through a human rights lens, gender equality in the WPS agenda was not considered pertinent to the security sector and therefore produced limited impact on high-level planning, operations, and military doctrines.

Finally, the lack of engagement with gender equality as an issue with security connotations may have also silenced the legacy of violence against minority groups. While the NAPs have been utilized as a platform to advocate for the rights of these marginalized groups, as well as to educate the security sector on the impact of conflicts on Indigenous and Moro women, thus far they have not been allowed to tackle the root causes of the conflicts and state-based violence, against the very promise of the human rights paradigm to address the deepest structural causes of discrimination and violence (see chapter 1). Both the National Commission on Indigenous Peoples and the National Commission on Muslim Filipinos noted the short-sighted impact of the WPS agenda. Research conducted in the Philippines has similarly revealed that one of the major problems with the NAPs has been "the failure to address the grievances of affected populations" (Amling et al. 2016, 30). The commissions envisaged the NAPs to investigate the drivers of armed conflict and security crisis in the Philippines, or in the words of NCIP, "the deep root causes of the war," such as limited land rights or access to resources for Indigenous peoples that have profound gender implications (NCIP, interview). Yet these issues were perceived as too political to be included in the NAPs. A representative from the NCMF also maintained that "while the NAP is prominent, it is still very limited in terms of its scope" (NCMF, interview), pointing out similar issues. Consequently, both NCMF and NCIP have continued to advocate for the rights of minority women, although without any strong references to the legacy of past and ongoing conflicts that are too controversial to be tackled in the context of NAP implementation. That state-based violence remains under the veil in the context of the NAPs was further confirmed by the limited involvement of the Department of Justice and the Commission on Human Rights, whose functions have been crippled under Duterte's populist-nationalist regime.

In all of this, stabilizing the meaning of *gender equality* in line with the human rights paradigm has created certain opportunities for a meangful change. Yet it has also raised certain challenges, as evident from the Philippines case study. The next chapter will discuss the implementation of the WPS agenda by the government of Australia, where the NAP would be driven by a broad and inconsistent approach with elements of all three paradigms of gender equality.

Chapter 4

Government of Australia

Australia is recognized internationally as one of the global leaders on United Nations Security Council Resolution 1325 (UNSCR 1325) and the Women, Peace, and Security (WPS) agenda (Coomaraswamy 2015; Allen 2020). As a major donor to the Women's Peace and Humanitarian Fund, the global financing mechanism for the implementation of the agenda (UNDP 2021; see chapter 1 for more), and to development assistance more broadly (OECD 2021), Australia supported projects and programs in conflict-affected countries, most prominently in the region of Asia and the Pacific. At home, the "Australian National Action Plan on Women, Peace, and Security 2012–2019" (Government of Australia 2012), recently updated (Government of Australia 2021), provided the blueprint for the WPS policy. Gender equality remained at the heart of this policy. However, Australia's approach was largely incoherent and patchy in comparison with the Philippine case study discussed in the previous chapter, where the goal of gender equality was defined consistently across the policy and practice of the WPS agenda in line with human rights principles.

This chapter traces the operation of gender equality in the WPS agenda in the Australian case study to understand the implications and impact of a broad and inconsistent approach. Australia's first National Action Plan on WPS (NAP), concluded in 2019, was characterized by an encompassing discourse that demonstrated a nuanced gender analysis of peace and security efforts. This narrative embraced a range of issues around the safety, empowerment, and rights of conflict-affected women. These issues resonated with the security, development, and—perhaps most strongly—human rights paradigm of gender equality that emerged in the global WPS agenda, each offering a different understanding of the objectives related to women's *voices* and *experiences* in conflict prevention, conflict resolution, and post-conflict peacebuilding (see chapter 1). As chapter 1 detailed, the central feature of *the security paradigm of gender equality* was the emphasis on the protection of women from conflict-related violence and to a lesser extent on the participation of women in the security sector. *The development paradigm of gender equality* refocused the understanding of gender equality toward the gender-differentiated needs of women, especially in post-conflict recovery, as well as women's empowerment and participation in the context of peacebuilding. *The human rights paradigm of gender equality* called for greater attention to women's leadership and participation in all political processes and urged for respect for the rights of women.

With a nod to all three paradigms of gender equality, the sophisticated discourse of the Australian NAP subsequently failed to translate into a robust implementation strategy. The latter ended up significantly under-developed (see also Lee-Koo 2014; Lee-Koo 2016; Trojanowska 2019). Yet the broad approach to gender equality combined with the rudimentary implementation strategy led to some paradoxical consequences in the implementation practice. Government departments had the opportunity to interpret WPS objectives and redefine the goal of gender equality in line with one or more paradigms that suited their current institutional priorities. This resulted in significant policy development across the departments accountable to the NAP, especially in the security sector, where gender analysis had been historically neglected. At the same time, the overall implementation of the NAP was untargeted, and the impact on the ground is largely unknown. In other words, the incoherent approach to gender equality was followed by considerable traction of the WPS agenda across the government as a whole, yet the impact of it was relatively superficial.

This chapter draws from the analysis of the WPS policy in government departments over the lifespan of the first Australian NAP. The pronouncements of government and civil society representatives were juxtaposed with frameworks released at departmental levels to comply with the WPS agenda. Between 2016 and 2017, I interviewed sixteen policymakers and practitioners, including each government agency and department with responsibilities under the NAP (i.e., the Office for Women, the Department of Foreign Affairs and Trade, the Australian Defence Force, the Australian Civil-Military Centre, the Australian Federal Police, and the Attorney-General's Department) and Australia-based civil society organizations holding the government accountable to its WPS promises (i.e., members of the Australian Civil Society Coalition on Women, Peace, and Security). Additionally, I had the opportunity to directly engage in WPS policy and advocacy, while residing in Australia. I participated in government–civil society policy roundtables on UNSCR 1325 held between 2016 and 2019 in Canberra and Melbourne and contributed to shadow reporting of the government's implementation of the NAP (Jay et al. 2016; Trojanowska et al. 2018). I was also able to continue discussions of the WPS agenda with some of the major stakeholders, as part of a government-led community of practice conversation that informed Australia's second-generation NAP.

This chapter starts with the historical and political background to Australia's engagement with the WPS agenda, outlining the context in which the NAP had been developed and how this impacted its content and shape. I proceed to investigate the understanding of gender equality across the NAP and to what extent it was reflected in the implementation strategy. Thereafter, I explore the implementation practice of the government that followed the adoption of the NAP, looking specifically at the pursuit of gender equality by individual departments and agencies. In the conclusion, I bring together the empirical findings to discuss the completion of the first NAP and the role of gender equality in the next iteration, launched in April 2021.

THE WOMEN, PEACE, AND SECURITY AGENDA AND AUSTRALIA'S INTERNATIONAL REPUTATION

It is important to establish at the outset that the WPS agenda was perceived by the Australian government as an international rather than a domestic priority. Australia has not experienced armed conflict on its territory for decades (UCDP n.d.b), but the country has engaged in military interventions overseas, especially in the Middle East (including in Iraq and Afghanistan) and in assistance missions in the Pacific (including the Solomon Islands, Timor-Leste, Papua New Guinea, and Fiji; DFAT n.d.). Through these overseas operations Australia engaged with the WPS agenda most strongly. This had a profound impact on how gender equality would be conceived and pursued under the NAP.

NAPs have been the major mechanism for the global diffusion of the WPS agenda and national institutionalization of the agenda's objectives (True 2016; Tryggestad 2014; Miller et al. 2014). NAPs articulate the national policy of a given country in relation to UNSCR 1325. This policy may be domestic in case of inward-looking plans or foreign in case of outward-looking plans (Swaine 2017; Shepherd 2016). In Australia, UNSCR 1325 was deemed particularly relevant to foreign affairs, security and defence policy, and the development and aid program, as opposed to domestic politics. Ultimately, the NAP was predominantly outward-focused. In the context of Australia's socioeconomic and geopolitical status and economic resources, the outward-looking orientation of the NAP was somewhat intelligible. It is common for donor countries to adopt WPS policies that engage with foreign rather than domestic affairs and support conflict-affected countries through specific projects and programs (Miller et al. 2014).

Yet this outward-looking orientation distanced the Australian NAP from local challenges, making it quite abstract. Dunn (2014, 285) argued that the Australian NAP "has all but ignored the local context in its development and application, focusing instead on its commitments abroad." Researchers and activists alike criticized Australia's WPS policy for the lack of engagement with the colonial history of acquisition of the land and the lasting impact of violence on the Aboriginal and Torres Strait Islanders (Dunn 2014; see also Allen 2020), but even more so for the silencing of the situation of conflict-affected refugees seeking asylum in Australia (Jay et al. 2016; Lee-Koo 2018; Trojanowska 2019). Neither of these issues were included in the NAP. By the same token, gender equality in Australia's WPS policy was conceived as an objective that targeted women in conflict-affected countries, as opposed to conflict-affected women at home.

The external motivation behind the NAP was even more evident in how Australia's WPS policy came about. The adoption of the first Australian NAP in 2012 was driven by Australia's bid for a nonpermanent seat on the UN Security Council for the years 2013–2014. The NAP was a key element of the eventually successful campaign of the Australian government that emphasized the commitment to "advancing gender equality" (Lee-Koo 2014; Shepherd and True 2014). This was showcased through Australia's cosponsoring of earlier WPS resolutions (i.e., UNSCR 1820, 1888, 1889, and 1960) and precisely through the development of the NAP, which at the time of the campaign had been still underway. While the Australian government's interest in the WPS agenda may have been genuine—and it did appear genuine throughout my interviews, which will be presented later in this chapter—the Security Council's bid made the NAP a political priority and a means to goals other than gender equality, such as strengthening international reputation of Australia as a gender equality leader and expanding the political influence within the UN system.

Even though the final push for the NAP adoption coincided with the campaign for the Security Council's seat, Australian-based civil society organizations were lobbying the government from as early as 2008 (Mundkur and Shepherd 2018). Having secured government funding in 2009, the Australian branch of Women's International League for Peace and Freedom (WILPF Australia) and UN Women Australia conducted consultations in every Australian capital city to identify the community's interests and concerns pertaining to the WPS agenda (see Porter 2009). To complement these efforts, the Office for Women, Australia's national machinery for the advancement of gender equality, ran consultations with government departments and agencies to determine their priorities.

Envisaged as complementary processes, civil society and government consultations were eventually confused in time due to larger political events in 2010. In particular, the change of the then prime minister, Kevin Rudd, who was deposed and replaced by Julia Gillard, led to a cabinet reshuffle, and a bulk of the WPS work needed to restart under new ministers to secure their endorsement. As a result, the community consultations concluded over a year before the final government consultations began and had more limited impact on the shape of the NAP, which was in the end finalized in "a scramble," in the words of a government representative, due to the Security Council's bid. The NAP was launched on International Women's Day in 2012, but many of the civil society interviewees expressed disappointment with both the process and the outcome, especially the outward focus of the WPS policy.

NATIONAL ACTION PLAN ON WOMEN, PEACE, AND SECURITY

The external motivation that has driven Australia's engagement with UNSCR 1325 coupled with the confused NAP development process resulted in an uneven WPS policy across the narrative and the implementation framework. Generally, NAPs are two-part documents starting with an outline to the context of WPS implementation and priorities in a given country and ending with an implementation strategy with action points, roles and responsibilities, as well as monitoring and evaluation indicators. In the Australian case study, the broad and nuanced approach to gender equality presented in the narrative report contrasted with the implementation strategy, where the complexity of gender equality disappeared (Lee-Koo 2014; Lee-Koo 2016; Trojanowska 2019). Specifically, the NAP was a document inclusive of the views of multiple stakeholders who were consulted on its development, and it outlined a relatively broad conception of gender equality, resonating with security, development, and human rights paradigms of gender equality. Yet this sophisticated understanding of how gender equality operates in peace and security was followed by a simplistic implementation strategy.

The Australian NAP started with a nuanced narrative report that demonstrated a holistic approach to gender equality. While the NAP appeared to lack an overarching goal (see also HAG 2015), in part because the formulation was so broad and encompassing, it recognized the many dimensions of gender equality in relation to peace and security. The following extract provides an illustration of this strong discourse:

The benefits of advancing gender equality are far reaching and operate on a number of levels. Gender equality is essential for ensuring that women and girls' needs are met and human rights are protected, in times of both peace and conflict. It enables men to break away from often limiting and rigid gender roles and expectations of masculinity, which can be amplified in conflict-affected settings. It helps communities to raise healthier, better educated children and enhances countries' economic prosperity. Notably, equality between women and men is also a prerequisite for sustainable peace, security, and development. (Government of Australia 2012, 7)

This single extract—and there are many similar throughout the narrative report of the NAP, which is also the longest part—presented a solid case for gender equality in peace and security. It underscored the centrality of gender equality to the WPS agenda and combined features of all three paradigms of gender equality that emerged at the global level (see chapter 1). Yet it carefully avoided the weaknesses associated with each of them. In line with the security paradigm, a meaningful link was established in the NAP between equality on the one hand and sustainable peace and global stability on the other—but gender equality was not securitized or turned into a means to other objectives such as military effectiveness. Women's contribution to the prosperity of post-conflict nations was highlighted, as was the welfare of families and communities—in accordance with the development paradigm— but women's roles were not gender-stereotyped and the gender difference was not essentialized, as the NAP refrained from attributing inherent caretaking qualities to women. Rather, the policy noted the complexity of women's roles, stating that "women and girls are not only victims needing protection" but "also active agents in both perpetuating conflict and building peace" (Government of Australia 2012, 7). The intersectional nature of gender inequalities was also acknowledged when the NAP suggested that "women and girls are not a homogenous group" but "conflict affects diverse groups of women and girls in very different ways" (Government of Australia 2012, 6).

The gender analysis was far-reaching overall, pointing to the cross-cutting nature of gender equality, with women's rights and participation placed at the center stage. Just like in the global human rights paradigm of gender equality, which is the most pronounced paradigm in the narrative, the Australian NAP demonstrated some awareness of how inequalities do not arise in a vacuum but rather occur on a continuum between conflict and non-conflict situations. In this context, the NAP paid attention to the root causes of armed conflicts and structural violence, including the links between dominant masculinities and states' propensity toward violence. In all of this, the NAP capitalized on the potential of UNSCR 1325 for delivering a meaningful change, asserting that "the implementation of the Women, Peace, and Security agenda is a long-term and transformative piece of work" (Government of Australia 2012, 15).

The narrative report was the part of the NAP that bore the marks of engagement with the 2009 community consultations. The consultations' outcome report singled out gender equality as one of the central ingredients of the WPS agenda when emphasizing "the moral imperative [of Australia] to foster gender equality as part of this process" (Porter 2009, 8; see also Shaw et al. 2010). The strong narrative embedded in human rights principles and immersed in a comprehensive gender analysis, including of structural inequalities and power dynamics involved in peace and security, was praised by both feminist researchers and activists. For instance, Lee-Koo (2014, 304) commented that "the NAP advocates a sophisticated understanding of the gender politics of armed conflict," further recognizing "the central connections between gender equality and peace." As aptly concluded by a civil society representative, "The NAP does embed the principles of gender equality or tries to embed the principles of gender equality" (CSO 6, interview).

Sadly, the Australian NAP subsequently fell short in the attempt to translate this nuanced approach to gender equality into a robust framework for action and to operationalize the goal of gender equality in a meaningful way (see also Lee-Koo 2014; Lee-Koo 2016; Trojanowska 2019). What followed the lengthy narrative report was a brief action matrix and a simplistic monitoring and evaluation framework. Neither engaged with the nuanced discourse on gender equality. The five overarching strategies unpacked in twenty-four action points that are shared between government departments were generic and apparently driven by compliance with UNSCR 1325 rather than the goal of improving gender equality opportunities or outcomes more directly. The strategies called for integrating a gender perspective in peace and security policies, improving the recruitment and management of the military and police personnel to ensure greater gender balance in the security sector, supporting civil society organizations in promoting gender equality and women's participation, and promoting the WPS agenda at home, in the countries of concern for Australia and internationally through the UN (Government of Australia 2012, 21–25).

Yet there was little reflection on the gender analysis that was explicated so eloquently in the narrative report. Instead, the action matrix ended up reductive and superficial. This sentiment was evident among Australian civil society. The interviewee who praised the discourse embedding gender equality principles in the aforementioned excerpt did not hide the disappointment with implementation framework, stating, "The challenge I have with our NAP is that it's all very well[-written] in the preface. But there is that tension between conceptually recognizing something but not actually figuring out what that means in implementation" (CSO 6, interview). As the interviewee concluded, the nuanced understanding of gender equality "seems to go out of the window" in the implementation framework (CSO 6, interview).

If the action matrix of the NAP was simplistic, then the monitoring and evaluation framework was even less robust. Both the Interim Independent Review and the Final Independent Review, compiled by subject matter experts, dedicated a large portion of recommendations precisely to the monitoring and evaluation framework (HAG 2015; Hartley et al. 2018). This was a recurring issue also in the civil society reports assessing the Australian government's implementation of the WPS agenda, one of them calling the monitoring and evaluation framework "the single biggest failing of the first NAP" (Jay et al. 2016, 27). In comparison to early NAPs adopted in other countries (cf. Fritz et al. 2011; Miller et al. 2014; Trojanowska et al. 2018), it was positive that the Australian policy designed sixteen indicators that combined predominantly quantitative with some descriptive, quasi-qualitative measures. Yet these indicators were output-based and limited to "counting women" or "describing activities" without providing any tool to measure the actual impact of the NAP implementation. That is, the monitoring and evaluation framework tasked the implementing agencies with the collection of sex-disaggregated quantitative data such as the number of women and men employed by relevant government departments, the number of reported cases of sexual and gender-based violence allegedly perpetrated by Australian personnel deployed overseas, or qualitative data with description of policy documents or seminars and events referencing the WPS agenda in any capacity or context. As a result, it was determined that the monitoring and evaluation framework was "inadequate to measure the effectiveness of the NAP" (Wittwer in Hewitt 2017, 4). As Lee-Koo (2016, 345) explained, "It is impossible to gauge the feminist impact of these training activities without a qualitative analysis of their philosophy, quality and outcomes." As a matter of fact, it is impossible to gain a deeper understanding of any real-life impact of the NAP merely on the basis of the government's reporting against the monitoring and evaluation framework.

Indeed, the inadequacy of the monitoring and evaluation framework became even more evident in the voluminous NAP progress reports that were tabled in Parliament in 2014, 2017, and 2018 respectively. The first report released in 2014 consisted of descriptive and quantitative data without a reflection on the progress made on the ground, least of all the impact on gender equality, whether in Australia or in conflict-affected states, or at the very least in the operation of the relevant government departments. In recognition of these shortcomings, the 2016 and the 2018 editions demonstrated some effort to include more robust data on the implementation of the NAP's strategies, for example, through the incorporation of case studies (see PM&C 2017; 2018). However, those case studies were captured in an unsystematic manner (e.g., under some of the action items but not under other, without justification) and without assessment of the impact on conflict-affected women and environments. The progress reports listed numerous initiatives undertaken under the NAP, providing valuable baseline data and a track record of WPS activities undertaken by government departments, but a scrutiny of the actual change is missing. While this did not mean that there were no gender equality outcomes resulting from the broad array of activities of the Australian government, given the limitations of the monitoring and evaluation framework, there was no way of knowing the real-life impact of the NAP implementation beyond anecdotal evidence. Ultimately, as a guiding policy document, the Australian NAP—while informative and evidently dedicated to the goal of gender equality inclusive of the rights, safety, and well-being of women—presented only a weak instrument insufficient to create or account for an impact on the lived experience in conflict zones.

GOVERNMENT'S IMPLEMENTATION OF THE NATIONAL ACTION PLAN

The challenge to operationalize the WPS agenda, and especially the goal of gender equality, was not unique to Australia. Rather, it was noted in several countries worldwide in the first-generation NAPs (Swaine 2009; Trojanowska et al. 2018). In Australia, however, the uneven document across the narrative report and the framework for action led to paradoxical outcomes, including significant policy development in individual departments. The broad approach to gender equality evident in the NAP's narrative reflected the views of government departments and agencies in their diversity. As stated by an interviewee, "The departments . . . have different understandings of gender equality and they have been included in it [the NAP]" (CSO 5, interview). In the absence of a prescriptive implementation strategy, this broad approach to gender equality enabled the government's engagement with the WPS agenda across departments and agencies, who could tailor the agenda's objectives to their mandates and core business in line with one or more paradigms of gender equality, accounting for their different institutional interests and political priorities. The result of this was significant traction of the WPS agenda in departmental policies which promoted gender equality, whether as part of the WPS agenda or more broadly. But gender equality diffused in distinct ways, leading to inconsistent implementation practice both in individual departments and overall (see also Allen 2020). The rest of this chapter will zoom in on the implementation practice of government departments, starting with the Office for Women, which coordinated the NAP.

The Impact on the Peace and Security Agenda

The Office for Women (OFW) was "the custodian of the NAP" (OFW 2, interview). As a gender policymaking agency, the OFW contributes gender expertise across the Australian government (Harris Rimmer and Sawer 2016), and the WPS agenda was one of the many policy areas that fell under the portfolio of agency. In the implementation of the NAP, the role of the OFW was nonoperational but instead the agency oversaw and supported the work of other departments. The OFW did so through chairing the high-level Inter-Departmental Committee on Women, Peace, and Security and the lower-level Subcommittee on Women, Peace, and Security that jointly coordinated the NAP implementation of the government, compiling periodic reports and liaising with civil society organizations in Australia to ensure their input was considered by the implementing departments.

In this unique role in the NAP, the OFW emphasized the centrality of gender equality to the realization of UNSCR 1325's goals. When asked about what gender equality means in the context of peace and security, an interviewed representative asserted the following:

> From the OFW's perspective, we know that women are disproportionately represented amongst the most poor, marginalized people in Australia and in the world. We know that gender inequality is a source of violence against women, including systematic violence. We know that women's economic inequality, women and children not being safe and being subjected to violence, [and] the exclusion of women from decision-making roles are all expressions of fundamental gender inequality and denial of women's human rights. The WPS goals are really about recognizing that this as a set of circumstances means that conflicts play out very differently for women and girls from men. (OFW 2, interview)

It was evident during the interview with the OFW that the agency had significant expertise in gender equality policymaking. The representative repeatedly advocated for a holistic understanding of gender equality, inclusive of multiple and intertwined aspects, be they sociopolitical and economic conditions or rights and safety of women, resonating with all three paradigms of gender equality focused on security, development, and human rights. This approach was informed by a gender analysis that shed light on the impact of structural discrimination and violence on the status of women in Australia and worldwide, including women in conflict-affected countries. These views reinforced the broad approach to gender equality articulated in the NAP's narrative report. They further supported the inclusion of a variety of gender equality issues to be considered by government departments in their implementation of the NAP.

Despite the depth of the gender expertise showcased by the OFW, the agency was historically less exposed to foreign affairs, security and defense, or development and aid, which were the key areas of the outward-looking NAP. The primary focus of the OFW's work revolved around a domestically oriented set of problems such as economic empowerment of women in Australia and especially family violence in line with Australia's long-standing domestic policy articulated in "National Plan to Reduce Violence against Women and their Children 2010–2022" (COAG 2011). Moreover, at the time of the NAP adoption in 2012, the OFW sat within the Department of Families, Housing, Community Services, and Indigenous Affairs (subsequently turned into the Department of Social Services), a domestically oriented service department, and had limited engagement with more powerful departments designated with the implementation of the NAP. Even though this changed shortly after the NAP was released when the OFW relocated back to the Department of the Prime Minister and Cabinet (PM&C) in 2013 (see also Harris Rimmer and Sawer 2016), the agency continued to exhibit limited authority over the NAP departments. In the context of the WPS agenda, the interviewed representative concluded that "it's very seldom that we have direct control over resources, outcomes or other agencies" (OFW 2, interview). As such, the OFW had little power to shape the peace and security agenda of the Australian government. This was in the hands of other departments.

The Impact on Foreign Affairs and Development and Aid Program

The Department of Foreign Affairs and Trade (DFAT) was envisaged as a major stakeholder in the Australian government operationalizing WPS objectives through concrete projects and programs. Co-responsible for twenty-one (out of twenty-four) action items under the NAP, DFAT's obligations distinctively related to the promotion of the WPS agenda in multilateral fora and in fragile, conflict-affected states. Despite the repeated cuts of the aid budget since 2013 (ANU 2021), the department continued to engage in a broad range of projects supporting gender equality goals internationally through the UN system and regionally in Asia and the Pacific. UNSCR 1325 fit easily into the preexisting policy environment, providing additional impetus for DFAT's gender equality work centered around women's leadership in conflict and post-conflict settings. As evident in the advocacy, policies, and pronouncements of DFAT's representatives, the human rights paradigm of gender equality framed the department's engagement with the WPS agenda, enhancing preexisting commitments but eventually also limiting the impact of UNSCR 1325 on Australia's foreign policy.

Just like in the global human rights paradigm of gender equality, women's participation and decision-making were at the heart of DFAT's approach to the WPS agenda. When a member of the Security Council in 2013–2014, it was argued that Australia adopted a distinct perspective on the WPS agenda (Shepherd and True 2014, 261). Other self-proclaimed global leaders on UNSCR 1325, such as the United States and the United Kingdom, emphasized protection from conflict-related sexual violence (e.g., through the United Kingdom's Preventing Sexual Violence Initiative), engaging with the security paradigm of gender equality most strongly. Australia, by comparison, advocated for women's rights more directly.

During the presidency of the Security Council in September 2013, Australia cohosted the High-Level Panel on Women's Participation in Peacebuilding, and in the same month, led the work on UNSCR 2117 on small arms and light weapons, the resolution that subsequently integrated substantive language on "women's full and meaningful participation in all policymaking, planning and implementation processes to combat and eradicate the illicit transfer [of weapons]" (S/RES/2117, OP 12) (see also Shepherd 2017). A civil society representative commented on this resolution by saying that "it could well be that without Australia's leadership on that issue, UNSCR 2117 would have gone without any recognition that women and girls suffered disproportionately from the violence caused by the flows of small arms and light weapons" (CSO 7, interview). Furthermore, in 2014 Australia secured gender-sensitive language in UNSCR 2145 (S/RES/2145) on the extension of the mandate of the UN Assistance Mission in Afghanistan. Australia's achievements during its term at the Security Council prompted a government representative to assert in an interview that, internationally, Australia "can provide real leadership and one of the issues that we've been known for leadership on is gender equality" (ACMC, interview).

The traction of the WPS agenda continued in DFAT beyond the Security Council membership. The Gender Equality and Women's Empowerment Strategy (Gender Strategy), released in 2016, provided more specificity and focus to the department's implementation of the NAP through projects and programs in conflict and disaster-affected countries. The Gender Strategy guides the incorporation of gender equality across all work of DFAT (i.e., foreign policy, economic diplomacy, development and aid program, and human resource management), not limited to the WPS agenda. It touched on issues ranging from women's economic empowerment through ending violence against women to enhancing women's voices in decision-making, leadership, and peacebuilding (DFAT 2016, 5). WPS obligations were once more clustered under the priority area dedicated to women's participation and leadership, strengthening the link between UNSCR 1325 and the human rights discourse. The Gender Strategy explicitly stipulated that DFAT would "promote women's participation in decision-making in response and recovery efforts" and "ensure that women participate effectively at all stages of peace processes and reconstruction" (DFAT 2016, 7). A department representative stated that in emphasizing women's leadership and participation in processes related to conflict prevention, conflict resolution, and post-conflict peacebuilding, the NAP "provided a platform [for DFAT] to speak about gender equality and to encourage other countries to do better on gender equality" (DFAT 3, interview).

Whether on the Security Council or in fragile, conflict-affected states, the NAP was utilized by DFAT to advocate for gender equality, approached through a human rights lens. The WPS agenda resonated with preexisting knowledge and culture within the department rather than initiating this advocacy from scratch (DFAT 1 and 2, interview). That the NAP alone was not the driver but only an additional platform to promote gender equality through the UN and in partner countries, became evident in the 2017 Foreign Policy White Paper. The Foreign Policy White Paper provides the roadmap to advance and protect Australia's national and international interests (DFAT 2017). This first white paper released since 2003 missed the opportunity to mention UNSCR 1325 in any capacity, despite overall and unprecedented attention to gender equality (Agius and Mundkur 2020), which was primarily perceived as a developmental issue (DFAT 2017, 93) rather than a human rights principle.

The Impact on Effectiveness and Culture of the Security Sector

Next to DFAT, the Department of Defence and the Australian Federal Police (AFP) are the other major government agencies implementing the NAP. Of the twenty-four-action items, the Australian Defence Force (ADF) and the Australian Civil-Military Centre (ACMC) (both falling under the Department of Defence, the latter being a whole-of-government agency overseeing civil-military-police capabilities in conflict and disaster management) contributed to seventeen and the AFP to fifteen (Government of Australia 2012, 21–25). Their primary responsibilities pertained to incorporating UNSCR 1325 into policies and operations along with embedding WPS principles into human resource management of the military and police forces. Overall, significant progress was noted across the former while the human resource management was rather neglected in the implementation of the NAP. In other words, WPS implementation has been founded on the integration of a gender perspective into international operations and in line with the security paradigm, the importance of gender equality was emphasized in relation to the effectiveness of offshore missions.

Despite being initially "oblivious" to the NAP, to use the words of an interviewee (ADF, interview), it is the AFP, but especially Defence, where progress was most notable and praised (e.g., Prescott et al. 2015; Allen 2020). Both developed distinct policies to comply with UNSCR 1325: the Defence Implementation Plan (Defence 2014, classified) and the AFP's International Deployment Group Gender Strategy (AFP 2014), later updated and turned into International Operations Gender Strategy 2018–2022 (AFP 2018). The purpose of these frameworks was to mainstream a gender perspective across policies, strategies, plans, and conduct of international operations. The Defence Implementation Plan was a classified, high-level operational security document, but its function was stipulated as follows:

> [The Defence Implementation Plan] includes tasks which provide greater emphasis and focus on gender mainstreaming activities that align with international, UN, and NATO efforts to integrate [a] gender perspective into armed forces, military operations and missions, and planning processes and align with the intent of United Nations Security Council Resolution 1325 and related resolutions. (Defence 2014)

The AFP's Gender Strategy spelled out similar objectives, emphasizing gender equality as "a core principle" that is "critical to achieving our mission of policing for a safer Australia" (AFP 2018, 4). It went on to assert that "gender diversity . . . allow[s] IO [International Operations] to build community trust, and strengthen our capacity to respond to local, national, and international challenges" (AFP 2018, 4). The term *gender diversity* referred to the inclusion of both women and men (as well as individuals from different cultural backgrounds) in police roles in international operations. Ultimately, the Defence Implementation Plan and the AFP's Gender Strategy alike centered the importance of gender equality around issues of operational effectiveness, aligning with the key themes of the security paradigm of gender equality.

The NAP filled an important gap in both the ADF and AFP. Traditionally, a gender perspective was neglected across their international portfolios. The WPS agenda provided a new and key tool to change this and advocate for gender equality for women (and men) in conflict-affected states where Australia operates. An ADF interviewee with an operational experience explained it in the following excerpt:

> Because we focus on the gender perspective part of UNSCR 1325, this has started to enable our people to understand the nexus between women's equality, their participation in public life and their participation in armed forces as being

an essential part of being successful in our peace and security efforts. (ADF, interview)

A representative from the ACMC reiterated this statement: "We have now arrived in a position when we consider gender mainstreaming as being a core human terrain issue of offshore operations" (ACMC, interview). In addition to the policy frameworks developed to comply with the WPS agenda, the Department of Defence created the post of the Director National Action Plan on Women, Peace, and Security within the Office of the Chief of the Defence Force. This was the first full-time high-level position in the Australian government appointed to facilitate the implementation of UNSCR 1325, confirming the importance of the WPS agenda to the security sector and Defence in particular.

Quite significantly, both the Defence Implementation Plan and the AFP's Gender Strategy impacted the implementation practice of the departments, translating the high-level objectives of the NAP into concrete institutional milestones on gender mainstreaming. In the ADF, the most significant gender equality advancements identified by interviewees were the introduction of Gender Advisors to offshore missions, starting with the 2013 deployment of Cap. Jennifer Wittwer to NATO's International Security Assistance Force to Afghanistan, as well as the integration of the WPS agenda into Australia's major military exercise, Talisman Sabre, from 2015 onward (AFD, interview; ACMC, interview). In a nutshell, the responsibility of Gender Advisors is to integrate a gender perspective into the conduct of military operations through assessing the implications of any planned activities on local women and men. Building on the success of the deployment of Cap. Witter to Kabul, the Australian government developed an Operational Gender Advisor Course, the only one of its kind in the Southern Hemisphere.

The inclusion of a gender perspective into Talisman Sabre was considered another major success attributed to the NAP. Talisman Sabre is a joint Australian and U.S. training activity in conduct of combined operations (see Defence n.d.). The integration of UNSCR 1325 in this exercise was called "an extraordinary achievement" of the Australian military. As explained by an ACMC representative:

In the initial phases . . . WPS was almost ruled out of contention a number of times, usually by mid-level American officers who went: What is this, it's a soft women's issue, we don't need to consider this. . . . At the end of the exercise when we were looking at what has been learned, we had the Commander of the US First Army Corps and the Commander of the US Specific Command (these are the most senior military people in the world!) turning around and saying: Well, one thing we've learnt from the Australians was the importance of having a gender perspective. (ACMC, interview)

The Australian NAP led to greater gender awareness in the security sector and specifically among personnel deployed to complex settings. It did so by emphasizing the critical importance of a gender perspective in building security in conflict-affected states where the ADF and the AFP operate. These achievements prompted Prescott and colleagues (2015, 6) to call Australia in their comparative NAP study "a model of a best practice for militaries to consider."

These critical advancements with respect to gender mainstreaming in ADF's and AFP's offshore operations contrasted rather starkly with problematic gender cultures identified at home. Even though Defence and the AFP were obliged under the NAP to "embed the Women, Peace, and Security agenda in the Australian Government's approach to human resource management" (Government of Australia 2012, 19), my empirical research found that this was applied merely to the international context of deployment. The human resource management of the staff at home bore no marks of engagement with UNSCR 1325, and this seemed even more perplexing given that the NAP implementation was underway in parallel to the "cultural reform" conducted within the ADF and the AFP in the aftermath of the 2011 "Skype scandal."

The Skype scandal was caused by publicized improper sexual behavior within the Australian Defence Force Academy. An academy's cadet, Daniel McDonald, secretly broadcasted via Skype the video of himself engaging in sexual activity with a female colleague who was unaware of and did not consent to being filmed. This scandal brought to the public scrutiny the situation of Australian uniformed women (see Defence 2017). A series of independent reviews into the treatment of women within the Australian security forces conducted by the former Australian sex discrimination commissioner, Elizabeth Broderick, revealed problematic gender cultures within both the ADF and the AFP, exposing the prevalence of sexual harassment and abuse within the security sector as well as the scarcity of opportunities for women to exercise leadership.

Despite evident overlaps between the cultural reform and the NAP, these two policies were systematically siloed. This was evident in the 2016 Defence White Paper, which, while referring to both UNSCR 1325 and the cultural reform, missed the opportunity to establish a meaningful connection between these two agendas and processes (Defence 2016). Rather surprisingly, I learned from the interviews with the departments that this was not an omission but a strategic decision. According to the ADF's representative:

> If we've started to make it a much bigger picture around women's equality and empowerment, we would just lose our people. They would start to think: It's

women's business, we are over it, it's not relevant to us. So, we had to tread a little bit carefully. . . . We've tried to do it in such a way that they understand the NAP as an operational imperative as opposed to those much more strategic goals around equality and empowerment of women. (ADF, interview)

An interviewee from the AFP confirmed this persistent separation of the cultural reform of the security sector and the WPS agenda, further pointing out that "in terms of the NAP and its implementation in the AFP, we've always struggled to get interest in it beyond the international operations portfolio" (AFP, interview).

While the decision to separate the WPS agenda from the cultural reform was prompted by a genuine desire for the NAP to be implemented, further scrutiny revealed that it negatively affected long-term gender equality efforts within the AFP and the ADF. The interviewed representatives unanimously complained about the lack of understanding of structural discrimination among most of their subordinates in these two massive institutions and the lack of a deeper understanding of how gender inequalities come about. A representative from the AFP stated:

Generally, there is not a good understanding of gender equality within the organization. There is limited understanding of gender equality in terms of the need to address equal/unequal [relations]. There is little appreciation of the structures that exist in the organization and have been created over a number of years that limit equal participation between the genders within the organization. (AFP, interview)

Decisions such as the one to detach the cultural reform from the NAP sustained—and might have at times exacerbated—systemic knowledge gaps with regards to gender equality as a fundamental human rights issue. Overall, security personnel reportedly lacked awareness of persistent structural inequality within the sector and how it affected uniformed women in Australia as well as local women in conflict-affected countries (see also Harris Rimmer 2016; Shepherd 2016). The security paradigm led to a very narrow understanding of gender equality and constrained the implementation of the NAP. Hewitt (2017, 7) similarly concluded her interview with Cap. Wittwer from the ADF with a conviction that "broadening our understanding of gender equality and WPS, what it is and why it matters is essential to overcoming impediments to successful implementation." Later years saw efforts to align the cultural reform more explicitly with the WPS agenda (e.g., AFP 2018, 9), yet the progress in implementing gender equality through the WPS agenda—while significant—continued to be uneven between international and domestic portfolios.

The Impact on Law and Justice

How the security paradigm of gender equality can result in constrained implementation of the WPS agenda was even more apparent in the last government department accountable to the NAP, the Attorney-General's Department (AGD). Even though the AGD was responsible for merely three action points under the NAP, I noted the explicit resistance toward the incorporation of WPS objectives across the work of the department in any capacity. As per mandate, the AGD oversees Australia's law and justice frameworks, whether at home or overseas, the latter through the prominent Pacific law and justice program (see AGD n.d.). With this role in mind, the AGD was included as an implementing agency under the current NAP. Moreover, with the emerging security challenges that intersect with the WPS agenda and sit within remit of the AGD, such as violent extremism, the pertinence of the WPS agenda was palpable. Yet no departmental-level framework was established throughout the lifespan of the NAP to comply with or support the implementation of UNSCR 1325. Instead, the shadow reporting of the NAP asserted that "civil society remains disappointed with the apparent low level of engagement by the Attorney General's Department with the WPS agenda" (Jay et al. 2016, 14). In an interview with the AGD, I was able to connect this resistance with the department's understanding of the WPS agenda and specifically a securitized approach to gender equality within it.

I quickly realized during the interview with the AGD that the department was not ignorant of the NAP or the WPS agenda. On the contrary, the interviewee demonstrated technical knowledge of WPS resolutions, the NAP, as well as the AGD's responsibilities that fell under it. Yet the agenda was essentially perceived as not applicable to the AGD's core business because the department did not operate in narrowly defined "conflict-affected" countries (i.e., countries that are currently on the Security Council's agenda). The interviewee admitted at the very start of our conversation that WPS-related work in the AGD is "pretty much nonexistent" (AGD, interview). With regards to the action items explicitly assigned to the department under the NAP's action matrix, the representative reacted by saying:

> Because we don't work in the conflict-affected or post-conflict countries, there is actually nothing to do to give effect to that. So, we do it by doing nothing because there is no policy framework that could apply to it. . . . There is nothing other than being aware of what other government agencies are doing. There is nothing in particular for us to contribute to that either. (AGD, interview)

The AGD established a strong track record on the protection of human rights in fragile countries of Asia and especially the Pacific. A variety of department-led programs supported gender equality efforts including through ongoing assistance to Papua New Guinea, the Solomon Islands, Kiribati, Tuvalu, and the Cook Islands, where the AGD contributed to developing policy legislations on women's rights and protection from gender-based violence. But these initiatives were not prompted or even affected by the NAP to any extent, reportedly. Despite strong preexisting frameworks on gender justice, embedded in human rights principles, the AGD adopted a securitized approach to UNSCR 1325 and consequently ruled out its relevance. This went far enough for the representative to contemplate whether the AGD should be involved at all in Australia's second NAP in any way. Paradoxically, the broad and inclusive gender equality discourse of the NAP enabled the AGD to select a narrow, securitized, and legalistic approach and disengagement with the WPS agenda.

Where the concept of gender equality did not diffuse through the WPS agenda, despite the pertinence, was the Department of Immigration and Border Protection, now integrated into the structures of the Department of Home Affairs. Neither in the narrative part nor in the implementation framework of the NAP was the department referred to, in any capacity. The department was therefore not included in Australia's WPS policy, and neither were conflict-affected refugees or asylum seekers in Australia. Australian civil society, however, was "unanimous in identifying conflict-affected women seeking asylum in Australia as falling within the remit of Australia's WPS obligations" (Jay et al. 2016, 21; see also Lee-Koo 2018). Protection of conflict-affected women from sexual violence or other human rights violations and the need to address their gender-differentiated needs in post-conflict recovery is clearly within the ambit of UNSCR 1325. But the department had no role in the development or implementation of the NAP.

CONCLUSION

This chapter speaks to the completion of the Australian NAP that expired with the end of 2019. The NAP reflected the deeply political process in which it was developed and gender equality interplayed with other political interests of the government. They included international priorities related to Australia's membership on the UN Security Council and regional priorities related to the implementation of the development and aid program and the conduct of security operations in countries where Australia operates. Some of these interests were only indirectly linked to the goal of gender equality, but all of them had implications for how gender equality was conceived by the Australian government in its engagement with the WPS agenda.

The result of these multiple priorities was an uneven document guiding Australia's implementation of the WPS agenda. The lengthy narrative part of the NAP demonstrated a strong commitment to a broad approach to gender equality, inclusive of security, development, and human rights issues. This discourse was founded on a nuanced gender analysis of conflict and post-conflict situations and was dedicated to delivering a transformative change in conflict-affected countries. However, while recognizing the complexity around gender equality at the conceptual level, the NAP failed to facilitate the translation of these transformative ambitions into a robust framework for action. The generic and reductionist implementation strategy, including the elusive accountability mechanism, was insufficient to result in or account for an impactful action. All these shortcomings left the decisions with regards to the implementation of the NAP in the hands of government departments, which could bargain for or against WPS priorities, aligning them with one of more of the paradigms of gender equality most suitable for departmental endeavors.

Consequently, the implementation of the WPS agenda took a vastly different course in the major government departments with operational tasks under the NAP, and there was significant variation in how gender equality was pursued. In the absence of clear directions in the NAP itself or from the Office for Women, which generally exhibited limited authority over powerful government departments responsible for foreign and security politics, the implementers had the opportunity to negotiate gender equality priorities of the WPS agenda with their departmental objectives. In the Department of Foreign Affairs and Trade, the approach to gender equality resonated most strongly with human rights principles, and the NAP provided an additional incentive for gender equality efforts that had been ongoing. While the WPS agenda diffused relatively broadly—easily connecting with preexisting polices and the organizational culture—it was slowly deprioritized after Australia concluded the Security Council's nonpermanent membership in 2014. This was evident in the lack of mentions to the WPS agenda in the 2017 Foreign Policy White Paper (see also Agius and Mundkur 2020).

By contrast, the Australian Defence Force and the Australian Federal Police both utilized the WPS agenda to fill an important gap in international policy and operations with regards to gender mainstreaming, aligning with the security paradigm of gender equality. These departments demonstrated perhaps the most palpable progress in the NAP implementation, specifically through international operations. New frameworks and policies were put in place to comply with UNSCR 1325.

Domestically, however, the influence of the WPS agenda on the human resource management of the security agencies was negligible, and the links between the NAP and the cultural reform of the security sector were

underemphasized. The overall gender awareness among security personnel remained limited beyond a narrow conception of gender equality as an
issue of operational effectiveness. The Attorney-General's Department also
adopted a security—or rather securitised—approach to gender equality, yet
it resulted in ruling the NAP out of contention, as the department declared
UNSCR 1325 to be irrelevant its core business. Even more disappointing
was the lack of involvement of Department of Home Affairs and the systemic exclusion of conflict-affected refugees and asylum seekers living in
Australia's jurisdiction, which reinforced preexisting inequalities and persistent silences around the situation of these women.

All in all, the NAP entailed significant policy development across the government. The broad narrative that was inclusive of different views on gender
equality and the lack of precision around the implementation strategy enabled
this policy development. Simultaneously, however, it constrained the possibilities for meaningful impact on long-term gender equality due to untargeted
implementation. Allen (2020, 4) similarly pointed to "significant inconsisten-
cies and resourcing gaps in how it [Australia] approaches the implementation
of its commitments on WPS." Nonetheless, the first Australian NAP laid
the foundation for the second iteration. Under the leadership of the Office
for Women and with support from the Australian Civil Society Coalition
on Women, Peace, and Security, the Australian government took the task
of developing the next iteration seriously and treated it as an opportunity to
address the shortcoming of the first NAP. Gender equality was placed at the
center stage of a discussion paper, which stated explicitly that it "should be at
the forefront of what governments do to prevent conflict, respond to national
disasters, and contribute to peacekeeping and peacebuilding" (OFW 2018, 2).
The draft of the second NAP was reportedly finalized in mid-2019, following eighteen months of extensive consultations, but the progress stalled until
2021, in part due to the Australian government's preoccupation with COVID-
19. Long overdue, the "Australian National Action Plan on Women, Peace,
and Security 2021–2031" was finally launched in April 2021.

The second-generation Australian NAP repeats some of the challenges of
the previous iteration but also demonstrates some improvements. The discourse on gender equality remains sophisticated and broad, but the issues of
WPS are perhaps more tangible, as they are more directly linked to case studies from Asia and the Pacific. The human rights paradigm is explicit in the
second iteration, not only through the four high-level outcomes (i.e., supporting women's meaningful participation and needs in peace processes; reducing
sexual and gender-based violence; supporting resilience, crisis, security, law,
and justice efforts to meet the needs and rights of all women and girls; and
demonstrating leadership and accountability for WPS) but also through the
adoption of "a human rights-based approach" as one of the guiding principles

(Government of Australia 2021, 10). The high-level monitoring and evaluation framework, while certainly improved from the first NAP and more meaningful in capturing the change related to WPS implementation, remains quite unspecific and unfocused. However, implementing departments are expected to develop departmental-level plans to operationalize the high-level indicators from the monitoring and evaluation framework.

There have been some changes with regards to implementing departments as well. Most significantly, the ownership of the NAP has moved from the Office for Women, which was under-resourced in the context of the WPS implementation, to the Department of Foreign Affairs and Trade and is to be led by the minister for foreign affairs. The Attorney-General's Department is no longer a party to the NAP, but the Department of Home Affairs has now been included. As Australian NAP expert Katrina Lee-Koo concluded:

> With focus on a human-rights based approach, a commitment to women's participation and gender equality, and an intention to show global leadership on the issue, the ingredients are there for a transformative impact. What it now needs is clear, consistent and focused leadership—backed by strong political will and resourcing—to use the NAP as a launching pad for Australia's WPS efforts. (Monash Gender, Peace, and Security Centre 2021, 5)

We have yet to see how meaningful the changes in the second-generation NAP will be and whether they will lead to targeted implementation and real-life impact on gender equality of conflict-affected women in Australia and overseas.

Conclusion

Transformative Politics of the Women, Peace, and Security Agenda

The purpose of this book was to explore how a core concept of feminist theory and a central incentive of feminist practice—gender equality—operates in arguably the most masculinist field of policymaking and governance: peace and security. The coupling of violent conflict with male-dominated security institutions has made the peace and security sector the epicenter of power-making, where issues of gender equality have been historically neglected. Set on the international peace and security agenda with the adoption of United Nations Security Council Resolution 1325 (UNSCR 1325) in 2000 and the inception of the Women, Peace, and Security (WPS) agenda, gender equality has become a key, albeit contested, goal in peace and security policy and practice. The resolution was a result of tireless feminist advocacy efforts and the work of bureaucrats and researchers across the globe, most importantly in conflict-affected countries. As such, it was celebrated internationally as the Security Council's first high-level acknowledgment of the relevance of gender equality to the promotion and maintenance of peace and security. However, the WPS agenda has over time become a site of contestation from both security institutions (that have questioned the placement of the objective of gender equality within the peace and security sector) and feminist advocates (who have expressed their concerns about the capacity of security institutions to support gender equality in meaningful ways) (see also True and Wiener 2019).

Personally, I have been both exhilarated and troubled by UNSCR 1325 and the developments that have occurred around the WPS agenda at the global, regional, and national level over the past two decades. I have been exhilarated because such a resolution, immersed in gender equality principles, is not a conventional outcome of the UN Security Council's patriarchal deliberations. UNSCR 1325 was a breakthrough in bringing the goal of gender equality to peace and security debates at the highest levels, and the traction of the WPS agenda has been significant within and beyond the UN system. But I have also been deeply troubled by the masculinist environment in which UNSCR 1325 and the subsequent resolutions emerged and what purposes they have been put up to serve, whether by the Security Council, regional organizations, or national governments across the globe, and whom the WPS agenda has benefited most as a consequence. This masculinist environment has influenced how the goal of gender equality has been conceived and pursued, yielding important implications for the implementation of the WPS agenda and for the impact it has produced on the ground (or in some instances, lack thereof). Over the years, I have continued to ponder how far and in what ways the WPS agenda can encourage the peace and security sector to genuinely seek gender equality, and what this may look like across policy and practice. This book is a result of empirical research guided by this questioning and driven by "feminist curiosity" defined as a grounded form of inquiry preoccupied with power imbalances and centered around women's lives (Enloe 2004).

Despite being a key policy goal of the WPS agenda, gender equality was underexamined in this context, remaining a major conceptual gap in international WPS research. Drawing on the empirical research and especially on expert insights of nearly seventy high-level stakeholders, including UN, government, and civil society actors, this book has started filling this crucial gap. In doing so, it has also intended to work toward bridging the epistemic siloes between international relations, where WPS research is primarily located, and gender studies, where theorizing of gender equality is traditionally undertaken. Through the nested case studies of the UN Security Council (chapter 1), the Association of Southeast Asian Nations and the Pacific Islands Forum (chapter 2), and the governments of the Philippines and Australia (chapters 3 and 4 respectively), I have aimed to disentangle the meaning and purpose of gender equality in institutions' engagement with the WPS agenda. The broad sweep of the book has additionally set out to unravel the complexity of the pursuit of gender equality at the juncture of the global and the local, pointing to how the implementation of the WPS agenda is intertwined with multiple political and institutional priorities and processes, including issues of international reputation, regional security, national sovereignty, and civil society advocacy.

Findings of this multilevel interrogation of gender equality, how it has shaped and has been shaped by peace and security policy and practice, were often ambiguous and sometimes paradoxical. Through the empirical chapters, I identified multiple possibilities and limitations embedded in the gender equality politics of the WPS agenda at the intersection of the global, regional, and national governance. This concluding chapter brings together the theoretical and empirical insights around the goal of gender equality in peace and security. It also traces implications for the political struggle for gender equality, for WPS policymaking, and for future research.

NO UNIVERSAL GOAL OF GENDER EQUALITY

I have begun and concluded my journey of writing this book with the understanding that the goal of gender equality is not easily grasped. An anthropologist raised a profound question: "Is it at all possible to talk about gender equality as a universal norm, unconditionally fixed, independent of historical and cultural context?" (Østebø 2015, 443; see also Østebø and Haukanes 2016). The answer to this question that has emerged in my empirical research is: probably not. Gender equality was evidently fluid in what it represented and how it operated. As an unfixed policy goal, the meaning and purpose of gender equality was context-specific and dependent on policy environments and coexisting and competing political and institutional interests. But while the goal of gender equality at times appears somewhat elusive, the impact of gender equality policies and programs can be very real and tangible.

Capturing gender equality in the context of peace and security, what it means, and how it can be attained turned out even more challenging than in other areas of policy and practice. Prior to UNSCR 1325, gender equality had been a foreign concept to the UN Security Council and to the peace and security sector at large. Despite mentioning it in passing and increasingly so over the years, neither UNSCR 1325 nor any of the nine subsequent resolutions adopted by the Security Council under the WPS banner (i.e., UNSCRs 1820, 1888, 1889, 1960, 2106, 2122, 2242, 2467, and 2493) provided a proxy for gender equality. On the contrary, the goal of gender equality has been smuggled into the Security Council's mandate and patriarchal decision-making structures.

When faced with the question of what gender equality is or should be in relation to peace and security, high-level stakeholders, whether UN, government, or civil society actors interviewed for my study, were commonly perplexed. Even though the vast majority endorsed the importance of gender equality to the WPS agenda, many of them placing it at the heart of UNSCR 1325, its meaning was commonly taken for granted. One of my interviewees maintained that gender equality was the end goal of the WPS agenda in the quotation that has become the epigraph of this book, "That's the end goal: if we succeed with the implementation of the Women, Peace, and Security agenda as it is laid out in the resolutions, the end goal will be gender equality" (UN, interview). When asked for more details, the interviewee admitted after reflection: "I haven't really given it that much of a thought." Many senior officials and WPS experts I had the privilege to discuss gender equality with had difficulties in explaining what the term conveyed. They did, however, have a great sense of how multiple sources of inequality have been embedded in current peace and security efforts, often to a detriment of conflict-affected populations, especially women and other marginalized groups.

My interviewees were among the implementers of UNSCR 1325 and often among the designers of WPS infrastructure and related programs in their respective institutions. Their support—but, even more so, their understanding—of gender equality is therefore not confined to their personal views, but it also impacts the institutionalization of the WPS agenda and the outcomes it produces through implementation. After all, "how we read UNSCR 1325 determines priorities," as Lee-Koo (2016, 337) aptly pointed out. This book has been deeply preoccupied with untangling the goal of gender equality in relation to peace and security priorities as outlined in the WPS agenda and manifested through its implementation at the global, regional, and national levels.

POLICY IMPLICATIONS OF PARADIGMS OF GENDER EQUALITY

My interrogation started with locating the overarching vision of gender equality in UNSCR 1325. In the absence of explicit mentions of *gender equality* in the body of the resolution, I relied on two objectives laid out in UNSCR 1325 that distinguished it from any previous effort of the Security Council when gender equality is considered. They concerned women's *voices* in conflict prevention, conflict-resolution, and post-conflict peacebuilding, and women's *experiences* of conflict and insecurity. Specifically, UNSCR 1325 called for an increased participation and representation of women in multiple roles across the peace and security sector, further recognizing the distinct impact of armed conflicts and security challenges on women and the need for appropriate response. These two intertwined objectives echoed the frameworks of equal opportunities, equal outcomes, and gender mainstreaming, and as such provided the blueprint for the conceptualization of gender equality that was elaborated in nine subsequent resolutions on WPS. But they have also entailed some of the key problems of gender equality policymaking, whether co-optation, assimilation, or essentialism.

UNSCR 1325's vision of gender equality was relatively broad, and this had important implications for WPS policy and practice and for the political struggle for gender equality. The objectives around women's voices and experiences were rather unspecific in terms of their scope and ramifications. Through the juxtaposition of policy analysis with expert interviews, my research indicated the coexistence of three paradigms of gender equality in operation with the WPS agenda. Originating from the pillars of the UN system, each paradigm offered a distinct reading of the two objectives and a different understanding of gender equality and further how it should be pursued, by whom and for whom.

The security paradigm of gender equality focused on the protection of women (and often children) from conflict-related sexual violence. It also called for the inclusion of women in the military and police roles to combat this hideous problem of many contemporary armed conflicts. *The development paradigm of gender equality* pinpointed the gender-differentiated needs in post-conflict recovery that stem from the distinct impact of armed conflicts on women. It further highlighted women's contributions to peace processes and peacebuilding. *The human rights paradigm of gender equality* emphasized women's participation and leadership in all political processes, without exclusion, and urged for the respect for women's human rights and protection from all forms of violence. By the same token, the human rights paradigm underscored the continuum of physical and structural violence as well as formal and informal participation across conflict, post-conflict, and non-conflict situations. But while the meaning and purpose of gender equality in each of the paradigms, and the strategy by which it was envisaged to be achieved, varied and this variation mattered greatly in terms of policy and practice implications of the WPS agenda, the advantages and disadvantages of the paradigms for the struggle for gender equality were less definitive.

The security, development, and human rights paradigms emerged directly from the empirical data and conceptualized gender equality as a cross-cutting policy goal. The paradigms have driven the institutional developments within the WPS agenda and underpinned related policy- and decision-making. That is, the paradigms have determined how gender equality has been operationalized and implemented by different institutions in various contexts. In the absence of a singular or established definition, WPS stakeholders have had the opportunity and convenience to align their understanding of gender equality with one or more of the paradigms that suited their political endeavors, even though these decisions may have not always been conscious. Consequently, the goal of gender equality has gained significant traction in WPS policy and practice, but at times it has been co-opted.

The broad remit of the WPS agenda has facilitated the diffusion of gender equality, including across political actors and agendas that previously had little to do with gender equality efforts, where the engagement with WPS policies has created a hook for an incremental change. Yet this lack of specificity has also pushed the WPS agenda in several directions, and gender equality has been sought in distinct—at times contradictory—ways based on different ideas, assumptions, and interests. Gender equality has been sometimes securitized, sometimes depoliticized, and its transformative potential has been sometimes diluted in the implementation practice. Ultimately, gender equality has gained prominence in peace and security through the WPS agenda and diffused across the sector; however, the broad vision of gender equality has also constrained the potential and actual impact of the agenda due to disjunctive policy development and patchy practice. The lack of coherence around the understanding of gender equality and how it relates to the WPS agenda has generated this dissonance and permitted the co-optation of this policy goal for other purposes.

While broad and unspecific on the one hand, the vision of gender equality outlined in the WPS agenda was simultaneously quite narrow and limiting. Across the paradigms, the scope of the WPS agenda confined gender equality to women's issues exclusively. The gender analysis has been ultimately limited, resonating with the commonplace risks of gender equality policymaking such as essentialism (i.e., a tendency to characterize women by a set of intrinsic qualities, attributes, and interests) and assimilation (i.e., a process that integrates women into preexisting structures that were created by and for men).

As I argued, the focus on women is crucial in the face of systemic discrimination and the invisibility of women's interests in global politics. The question of women deserves special attention particularly in peace and security where efforts toward greater gender equality should involve strategies that center around and elevate the voice and experience of women. Yet the WPS agenda at times appeared to have taken issues of gender equality out of the broader context of institutional structures and power dynamics that support and benefit from global inequality, and instead focused narrowly on women as apolitical subjects detached from that very context. As such, the WPS agenda has brought women to the peace and security discourse and practice, but it has often done so without challenging the deep structures of inequality entrenched in the peace and security sector that not only disadvantage and marginalize women but sometimes also threaten their safety and put their lives on the line. In this context, the prevalent misconceptions around understanding *gender* as synonymous with *women* has been a key limitation of WPS architecture (see also Hagen 2016, 317).

The lack of attention to gender (as a form of power that can be ascribed both to individuals and institutions) and the lack of reflection on inequality (as a form of power imbalance inherent in WPS resolutions and action plans) rendered invisible the role of men/masculinity and gender relations in conflict, in violence, and in sustaining global inequality. Both these together further invisibilized the insecurity of certain societal groups, particularly those affected by intersectional forms of violence and oppression, such as Indigenous peoples; racial or ethnic minorities; lesbian, gay, bisexual, transgender and queer minorities; young women; or women with disability. These marginalized groups may be specifically targeted in conflict and yet are often overlooked in post-conflict relief and recovery efforts. Their voices and experiences are mostly silenced throughout the WPS agenda that instead referred to "the universal woman" (Lee-Koo 2016, 337; see also Pratt 2013).

In all of this, the WPS agenda has exposed some of the persistent inequalities embedded in peace and security and created openings for the promotion of gender equality from within and from the outside of the sector. Simultaneously, it has sought to bring the goal of gender equality to the existing processes and structures without fundamentally challenging them or the inequalities they entail. Without engaging with and critically evaluating unequal gender power relations that prevail in peace and security policy- and decision-making, the WPS agenda has only been able to scratch the surface of patriarchy thus far. The limited gender analysis in the key gender equality debates within the WPS agenda constrained the possibility for a radical departure from masculinist identity and interests of the current peace and security sector and security institutions.

Ultimately, the vision of gender equality in UNSCR 1325 and the policy paradigms that emerged within the WPS agenda encapsulated major dilemmas of gender equality policymaking. The paradigms offered an opportunity to reevaluate pros and cons of key gender equality strategies, with a view to establish their relevance to WPS research as well as to international relations scholarship more broadly, and to trace their implications for policy and practice. Aligning with the pillars of the UN system, the paradigms also provided an analytical tool to understand gender equality as a cross-cutting objective in international politics, operating across the siloed areas of security, development, and human rights.

GENDER EQUALITY AT THE JUNCTURE OF GLOBAL, REGIONAL, AND NATIONAL GOVERNANCE

The ambivalences of gender equality policymaking in the WPS agenda and the tensions between the paradigms of gender equality were most palpable at the intersection of the global, regional, and national governance. Feminist advocates have long emphasized that in order to truly transform the experience of global inequality, the WPS agenda needs to translate from global promises to national accountability (e.g., Coomaraswamy 2015). WPS policies adopted at the regional and national levels were often a result of complex processes of negotiations between global and local actors, discourses, and practices, and the ambiguity of gender equality has been pronounced at this juncture, evoking historical power imbalances. The investigation of what occurs at the intersection of the global and the local engagements and the problematizing of inequalities that arise therein expose the invisibility of global inequality (e.g., Ackerly and Attanasi 2009). Below I bring together key findings from the empirical case studies located at the global, regional, and national level to reflect on where the implementation of the WPS agenda is heading.

At the global level, I could observe the growing friction between the security paradigm and the human rights paradigm within the institutional home to the WPS agenda, the UN Security Council. At the time of my field research at the UN Headquarters in 2015, there seemed to be a gradually formed agreement that the WPS agenda should be approached through a human rights lens even within the mandate of the Security Council. Yet in the following years, this understanding of gender equality has been increasingly resisted, with some of the Security Council's members locating it outside the council's ambit. Russia particularly, often backed up by China, has been the most vocal opponent of the human rights paradigm, even to the point of drafting, putting to vote, and failing to pass—on the twentieth anniversary of UNSCR 1325—a resolution that would backslide commitments to gender equality made in previous years and resolutions. The proposed resolution—that under the façade of addressing the impacts of COVID-19 on women in conflict-affected countries was designed to contain WPS issues within a narrow framework of security—was rejected by the majority of the council's members.

By the end of 2020, it became clear that the progress made over the years with respect to gender equality in global peace and security had been volatile and highly susceptible to processes and power dynamics within and outside the Security Council's chamber. This included the global backlash against women's rights. Simultaneously, it is a reason for optimism that as many as ten member states of the Security Council who abstained in the vote and delivered informed statements outlining their justifications, refused to undermine the gains from the past two decades in relation to women's human rights and civil society participation in WPS decision-making.

At the regional level, the WPS agenda interplayed with historical power imbalances and issues of colonialism experienced by Asia and the Pacific, as well as with the interactions of regional organizations with the UN system. The Association of Southeast Asian Nations (ASEAN) and the Pacific Islands Forum (PIF) both rejected securitized notions of gender equality prominent at the Security Council throughout the first decade of UNSCR 1325. I argued that the security paradigm of gender equality may have been associated with a threat to regional sovereignty rather than a means to greater gender equality. In lieu of employing the security paradigm, both ASEAN and the PIF engaged with the WPS agenda in distinct ways, connecting the WPS agenda to local security challenges and preexisting notions of gender equality.

Driven by the advocacy and entrepreneurship of local civil society, the PIF was relatively quick to develop a regional policy on WPS in 2012. The policy resonated with the human rights paradigm and presented a strong case for the rights and participation of women across the Pacific in the decision-making related to situations of conflict and post-conflict. UNSCR 1325 was utilized by civil society advocates to legitimize their efforts toward greater gender equality in peace and security. Sadly, there is little evidence of the implementation of this promising framework, and it appears that the WPS agenda has lost the momentum in the PIF in most recent years, with some of the key peace and security policies and events missing the opportunity to engage with UNSCR 1325.

By contrast, ASEAN's interest in the WPS agenda has been evident since 2017, despite the slow and somewhat reluctant start. Having opted for the development paradigm of gender equality, ASEAN has increasingly empha-sized the role of women in peacebuilding and their contribution to national prosperity. The pursuit of the WPS agenda has further accelerated with grow-ing interactions between ASEAN and the UN, including the release of the Plan of Action to Implement the Joint Declaration on Comprehensive Partnership between ASEAN and the United Nations (2021–2025) (ASEAN 2020; see also SC/14093). This culminated in ASEAN's public commitment to develop a regional plan of action on WPS in due course (ASEAN 2021, IV). In all of this, I used the case studies of ASEAN and the PIF and the trajectory of gender equality in the WPS agenda to reflect on issues that arise in gender equality politics at the juncture of global and regional policymaking—in addition to dilemmas common to gender equality policymaking globally.

At the national level, the case studies of the Philippines and Australia also illustrated distinct pathways—and sometimes bypasses—to gender equality through the WPS agenda. Having pioneered a national policy on WPS in the entire region of Asia and the Pacific in 2010, the Philippines presented a strong and consistent case of the human rights paradigm of gender equality that translated from policy to implementation practice. Moreover, the WPS agenda was integrated into preexisting human rights frameworks, securing ongoing implementation in line with earlier obliga-tions of the Philippine Government to the Convention on the Elimination of All Forms of Discrimination Against Women. These institutional develop-ments have enhanced efforts of certain government departments to mitigate the gendered effects of armed conflicts on women. Thanks to combining gender and conflict analysis, these departments have been better equipped to protect women's rights in conflict and post-conflict situations and to pro-vide gender assistance accordingly. Yet approached through a human rights lens, the WPS agenda and the notions of gender equality within it have been incongruent with the dominant militaristic security discourse. Consequently, the WPS agenda has had limited impact on the National Security Policy and the security sector in the Philippines, where the consideration of gender equality issues could perhaps have produced the greatest impact.

Some of the deepest root causes of violence and armed conflict have remained unaddressed, especially those that have to do with the systemic marginalization of minority groups, such as the Indigenous peoples and the Muslim population, who constitute the majority of conflict-affected people in the Philippines. State-based violence against those groups has for the most part been under the veil of the WPS agenda. The controversial presidency and hypermasculinist national leadership of Rodrigo Duterte, who has been in power since 2016, have not helped to fill those gaps. On the contrary, the WPS agenda appears to be at a high risk of being sidelined despite the ongoing security crisis in the Philippines, exacerbated by COVID-19.

Driven by international reputation and membership in the Security Council, Australia's engagement with the WPS agenda was more incoherent and marked by elements of all three paradigms of gender equality: security, development, and human rights. The inclusive and encompassing discourse on gender equality did not, however, translate down to the implementation strategy. The latter was reductionist and unnuanced. Interestingly, however, this had paradoxical consequences for the implementation of the WPS agenda by government departments and agencies. In the absence of a prescribed approach to the WPS implementation anchored in certain notions of gender equality, as was the case in the Philippines, individual departments were able to tailor their understanding of gender equality to their core business and corporate priorities. This resulted in significant—albeit uneven—policy development across the Australian government. The implementation of UNSCR 1325 took a vastly different course in and across departments with WPS responsibilities, with the security sector recording the most tangible progress, as the WPS agenda addressed a key gap in international operations around integrating a gender perspective. Yet in terms of domestic affairs, the impact of the WPS agenda was more negligible. The reluctance to address sexual abuse against uniformed women in Australia as part of the WPS agenda, as well as silences around and the systemic exclusion of refugee women and men or Indigenous peoples were persistent. The new WPS policy launched in 2021 after over a year-long hiatus is set to address some of these challenges through high-level commitment and concerted leadership.

Looking at the case studies of the UN Security Council, ASEAN and the PIF, and the governments of the Philippines and Australia, it is evident that the WPS agenda and the understanding and pursuit of gender equality within it have been influenced by political processes and events at the global, regional, and national levels. Some of them were directly linked to gender equality politics, while others were related to broader—but also gendered—security politics. Tendencies such as the global backlash against women's rights and the spread of national populism have affected the implementation of the WPS agenda as well as the adoption of or resistance to certain paradigms of gender equality. The prioritization—or more commonly deprioritization—of the WPS agenda has been also impacted by the COVID-19 pandemic. The problematic histories and presence of colonialism as well as imperialist tendencies have interplayed with attitudes toward the WPS agenda, sometimes leading to skepticism toward global discourses on gender equality. Recurring and emerging security crises, restrictions on civil society engagement, and issues of international reputation of states have been other factors that at times encouraged, at times discouraged, meaningful involvement of stakeholders in WPS implementation in different contexts and the buy-in (or sell-out) of the goal of gender equality by governments and regional and international organizations. All of these priorities have shaped the gender equality politics of the WPS agenda over the past twenty years, implicating which political subjects and which women and/or "others" have been most affected—or neglected—by the WPS agenda.

CONNECTING POLICY OBJECTIVES
WITH LIVED EXPERIENCE

Gender equality is perhaps the most critical analytical concept to "make feminist sense" of the WPS agenda and understand the ways in which UNSCR 1325 can bring about structural and real-life changes in peace and security. Throughout my multilevel investigation, gender equality has proven to be a cross-cutting objective in peace and security policymaking and governance. It has been fluid and this fluidity has created numerous opportunities, challenges, and risks for the implementation of the WPS agenda.

Rather than being the end goal of the WPS agenda that can be achieved once and for all, my empirically driven research concludes that the pursuit of gender equality is a complex project in which gains are often followed by setbacks and progress leads to resistance. Gender equality in operation with the WPS agenda is therefore an "unfinished business" and an inevitably contested process rather than a static outcome that can be pinned down. As a political—and not only policy—goal, gender equality still sits somewhat uncomfortably within the mandate of security institutions that continue to attempt to redelegate it outside the ambit of the peace and security sector. While feminist scholars (e.g., Flood et al. 2020) suggested that active resistance and even backlash against gender equality is a sign of progress that signifies engagement with the very idea of gender equality, such progress may be halted or reversed, and the momentum may be lost. To eventually become "business as usual" of the peace and security sector, gender equality requires continuous effort from policymakers, practitioners, activists, and researchers.

The question of gender equality in peace and security remains both timely and pressing. After all, gender equality—along with global peace and security—is perhaps one of the most undelivered promises of the UN system, regional organizations, and national governments. But two decades following the passing of UNSCR 1325, not only has gender equality not been achieved in peace and security, but it has also become a moving target. At the time of growing global instability related to the rise of violent extremism and terrorism, the polarization of political debates and growing incidence of political violence, natural disasters, health pandemics, including COVID-19, and humanitarian emergencies in countries such as Myanmar, Afghanistan, or Ukraine, gender equality has been increasingly put up to serve different purposes. The goal of gender equality, or sometimes the façade of it, has been instrumentalized toward various ends, not always retaining the feminist intent of UNSCR 1325. The policy paradigms of gender equality introduced in this book will hopefully provide a useful tool to monitor these processes as we move forward, with a view to understand their impact on the long-term political struggle for gender equality.

In the context of this rapidly changing geopolitical and institutional landscape and in the face of the deeply resistant to change patriarchal system we live and breathe, it is important to recognize that the concept of gender equality operates both at a normative and an empirical level. Normatively, gender equality is an objective of certain policies and laws (at the high-level) as well as programs and projects (on the ground), and as such it has been predominantly studied throughout the case study chapters of this book. How these policies and programs conceived and pursued gender equality varied from case to case. In this normative understanding, gender equality has been a key goal of WPS resolutions, policies, and action plans that typically centered around issues of women's voices in peace and security decision-making and women's experiences of conflict and post-conflict situations. Empirically, gender equality—or more commonly lack thereof—manifests through the diverse lived experiences of women (as well as men and "others"). The experience of violence or threat of violence, whether physical or structural, and the lack of voice or ability to exercise autonomy and self-determination in everyday life are common—perhaps the most common—features of contemporary armed conflicts and security crises. Moreover, this experience of gender inequality is often inseparable from other forms of oppression linked to race/ethnicity, indigeneity, sexuality, ability, socioeconomic status, education, and geographical location. After all, women from marginalized groups have been deeply affected by conflicts and insecurity, and yet they have often been silenced in WPS efforts.

This book attempted to combine the analysis of gender equality as a policy goal of the WPS agenda with the views of the stakeholders who have worked toward the realization of the agenda's objectives in various institutional settings. Some of the WPS policies I studied have been developed in top-down processes and served as political or demagogic tools to strengthen the reputation of security institutions or fulfil other political ambitions. By the same token, these policies did not always seek to connect with the lived experience of populations affected by armed violence and conflict-related insecurity. Some feminist researchers argued that in such cases, WPS policies may detract the peace and security sector from the long-term path toward gender equality (e.g., Swaine 2013; Basini and Ryan 2016). This is because the adoption of WPS initiatives is sometimes conceived as the end goal—rather than only the beginning—of the process of societal change. As such, the release of resolutions or the launch of action plans were sometimes treated as a "quick win" with no follow-up and even less follow-through.

Other WPS policies have been a result of bottom-up advocacy and tireless efforts of women's organizations and as such have been deeply informed by the lived experience of inequality. Yet some of them have failed to secure the buy-in from policymakers and institutions, and as such they have not translated into implementation practice. In those cases, WPS policies have not had a chance to bring about real-life changes despite the intent being there. Balancing the ambitious goals around gender equality with structural possibilities and limitations has been a key challenge to the successful implementation of the WPS agenda.

For a real change to occur in peace and security, the normative and empirical aspects of gender equality—the policy goal of gender equality and the lived experience—need to come into alignment and converge. I envisage the WPS agenda as a catalyst that, through the normative objective of gender equality, can transform the empirical experience of gender inequality toward that of being more peaceful, just, and equal. That is, the diverse lived experience ought to underpin the design and delivery of policies and programs, which should in turn change the lived experience toward greater gender equality as lived reality. The question of the extent to which this has been true for the WPS agenda thus far—whether gender equality as a policy goal of the WPS agenda has been informed by the lived experience of discrimination, oppression, and violence and has transformed it in return—was only touched on in this book. Yet it is a key conundrum for WPS researchers and practitioners in the third decade of UNSCR 1325.

Bibliography

Acharya, A. (2004). How ideas spread: Whose norms matter? Norm localization and institutional change in Asian regionalism. *International Organization, 58*(2), 239–275. doi:10.1017/S0020818304582024.

Acharya, A. (2005). Do norms and identity matter? Community and power in Southeast Asia's regional order. *Pacific Review, 18*(1), 95–118. doi:10.1080/09512740500047199.

Ackerly, B., & Attanasi, K. (2009). Global feminisms: Theory and ethics for studying gendered injustice. *New Political Science, 31*(4), 543–555. doi:10.1080/07393140903322604.

Ackerly, B., & True, J. (2008). Reflexivity in practice: Power and ethics in feminist research on international relations. *International Studies Review, 10*(4), 693–707. doi:10.1111/j.1468-2486.2008.00826.x.

Ackerly, B., & True, J. (2010). *Doing feminist research in political and social science.* Palgrave Macmillan.

Ackerly, B. A., Stern, M., & True, J. (2006). *Feminist methodologies for international relations.* Cambridge University Press.

Agius, C., & Mundkur, A. (2020). The Australian foreign policy white paper, gender and conflict prevention: Ties that don't bind. *Australian Journal of International Affairs, 74*(3), 282–300. doi:10.1080/10357718.2020.1744518.

Allen, L. (2020). *Australia's implementation of Women, Peace and Security: Promoting regional security.* Australian Strategic Policy Institute.

Allen, L., & Shepherd, L. (2019). *In pursuing a new resolution on sexual violence Security Council significantly undermines women's reproductive rights.* https://blogs.lse.ac.uk/wps/2019/04/25/in-pursuing-a-new-resolution-on-sexual-violence-security-council-significantly-undermines-womens-reproductive-rights.

Amling, A., Persinger, B., & Coolidge, K. (2016). The Philippines. In A. Amling & M. O'Reilly (Eds.), *From global promise to national action: Advancing Women, Peace and Security in the Democratic Republic of Congo, the Philippines, Serbia and Sierra Leone* (pp. 25–38). Inclusive Security.

Anderlini, S. N. (2007). *Women building peace: What they do, why it matters?* Lynne Rienner Publishers.

Anderlini, S. N. (2011). Translating global agreements into national and local commitments. In C. Oudraat, K. Kuehnast, & H. Hernes (Eds.), *Women and war: Power and protection in the 21st century* (pp. 19–36). U.S. Institute of Peace Press.

Anderlini, S. N. (2018). Civil society's leadership in adopting 1325 Resolution. In S. Davies & J. True (Eds.), *The Oxford handbook of Women, Peace, and Security* (pp. 38–52). Oxford University Press.

Association of Southeast Asian Nations (ASEAN). (1988). *Declaration of the advancement of women in the ASEAN region.* ASEAN.

Association of Southeast Asian Nations (ASEAN). (2015). *ASEAN regional plan of action on the elimination of violence against women.* ASEAN.

Association of Southeast Asian Nations (ASEAN). (2017). *Joint statement on promoting Women, Peace and Security in ASEAN.* ASEAN.

Association of Southeast Asian Nations (ASEAN). (2020). *Plan of action to implement the joint declaration on comprehensive partnership between ASEAN and the United Nations (2021–2025).* ASEAN.

Association of Southeast Asian Nations (ASEAN). (n.d.). *Association of Southeast Asian Nations.* https://asean.org

Association of Southeast Asian Nations (ASEAN). *ASEAN regional study on Women, Peace and Security.* ASEAN.

Association of Southeast Asian Nations Regional Forum (ARF). (2019). *Joint statement on promoting the Women, Peace and Security agenda.* ARF.

Australian Federal Police (AFP). (2014). *International Deployment Group's gender strategy.* AFP.

Australian Federal Police (AFP). (2018). *International operations gender strategy 2018–2022.* AFP.

Australian Government Attorney-General's Department (AGD). (n.d.). *Pacific law and justice program.* https://www.ag.gov.au/international-relations/pacific-law-and-justice-program

Australian Government Department of Defence (Defence). (2014). *National Action Plan on Women, Peace and Security: Defence implementation plan.* http://www.defence.gov.au/Women/NAP/ImplementationPlan.asp

Australian Government Department of Defence (Defence). (2016). *2016 defence white paper.* Australian Government Department of Defence.

Australian Government Department of Defence (Defence). (2017). *Pathway to change: Evolving defence culture.* https://www.defence.gov.au/pathwaytochange

Australian Government Department of Defence (Defence). (n.d.). *Talisman Sabre.* https://www.defence.gov.au/Exercises/TS15

Australian Government Department of Foreign Affairs and Trade (DFAT). (2016). *Gender equality and women's empowerment strategy.* DFAT.

Australian Government Department of Foreign Affairs and Trade (DFAT). (2017). *2017 foreign policy white paper.* DFAT.

Australian Government Department of Foreign Affairs and Trade (DFAT). (n.d.). *Australia's development program*. https://www.dfat.gov.au/development/australias -development-program

Australian Government Department of the Prime Minister and Cabinet (PM&C). (2014). *2014 progress report: Australian National Action Plan on Women, Peace and Security 2012–2018*. PM&C.

Australian Government Department of the Prime Minister and Cabinet (PM&C). (2017). *2016 progress report: Australian National Action Plan on Women, Peace and Security 2012–2018*. PM&C.

Australian Government Department of the Prime Minister and Cabinet (PM&C). (2018). *2018 progress report: Australian National Action Plan on Women, Peace and Security 2012–2018*. PM&C.

Australian Government Office for Women (OFW). (2018). *Discussion paper: Australia's second National Action Plan on Women, Peace and Security*. OFW.

Australian National University (ANU). (2021). *Australian aid tracker*. http://devpolicy.org/aidtracker

Autonomous Bougainville Government. (2016). *Policy for women's empowerment, gender equality and peace and security*. Autonomous Bougainville Government.

Bacchi, C., & Eveline, J. (2010). *Mainstreaming politics: Gendering practices and feminist theory*. University of Adelaide Press.

Barrow, A. (2016). Operationalizing Security Council Resolution 1325: The role of national action plans. *Journal of Conflict and Security Law, 21*(2), 247–275. doi:10.1093/jcsl/krw002.

Basini, H., & Ryan, C. (2016). National action plans as an obstacle to meaningful local ownership of UNSCR 1325 in Liberia and Sierra Leone. *International Political Science Review, 37*(3), 390–403. doi:10.1177/0192512116636121.

Basu, S. (2016a). Gender as national interest at the UN Security Council. *International Affairs, 92*(2), 255–273. doi:10.1111/1468-2346.12548.

Basu, S. (2016b). The Global South writes 1325 (too). *International Political Science Review, 37*(3), 362–374. doi:10.1177/0192512116642616.

Basu, S. (2018). Security Council Resolution 1325: Toward gender equality in peace and security policymaking. In B. Reardon & A. Hans (Eds.), *The gender imperative: Human security vs state security* (pp. 287–316). Routledge.

Bellamy, A. J., & Beeson, M. (2010). The responsibility to protect in Southeast Asia: Can ASEAN reconcile humanitarianism and sovereignty? *Asian Security, 6*(3), 262–279.

Bellamy, A. J., & Davies, S. E. (2009). The responsibility to protect in the Asia-Pacific region. *Security Dialogue, 40*(6), 547–574. doi:10.1080/14799855.2010.507414.

Benschop, Y., & Verloo, M. (2006). Sisyphus' sisters: Can gender mainstreaming escape the genderedness of organizations? *Journal of Gender Studies, 15*(1), 19–33. doi:10.1080/09589230500486884.

Bhagwan-Rolls, S. (2014). Thinking globally and acting locally: Linking Women, Peace and Security in the Pacific. In G. Heathcote & D. Otto (Eds.), *Rethinking peacekeeping, gender equality and collective security* (pp. 118–130). Palgrave Macmillan.

Bhagwan-Rolls, S., & Rolls, S. (2019). WPS and the Pacific Islands Forum. In S. Davies & J. True (Eds.), *The Oxford handbook of Women, Peace, and Security* (pp. 402–412). Oxford University Press.

Bhagwan-Rolls, S., & Stone, L. (2016). The role of women in regional peace and security. In D. Cortright, M. Greenberg, & L. Stone (Eds.), *Civil society, peace, and power* (pp. 143–158). Rowman & Littlefield.

Brown, W. (1995). *States of injury: Power and freedom in late modernity*. Princeton University Press.

Castillo Diaz, P., & Tordjman, S. (2012). *Women's participation in peace negotiations: Connections between presence and influence*. UN Women.

Celis, K., Childs, S., Kantola, J., & Krook, M. L. (2008). Rethinking women's substantive representation. *Representation, 44*(2), 99–110. doi:10.1080/00344890802079573

Charmaz, K. (2014). *Constructing grounded theory*. SAGE.

Chinkin, C., & Rees, M. (2019). UN Security Council Resolution 2467: Reasons for optimism. https://www.wilpf.org/un-security-council-resolution-2467-reasons-for-optimism

CNN Philippines. (2017). Duterte rejects EU aid yet again: "Forget it, we will survive." http://cnnphilippines.com/news/2017/11/15/asean-duterte-rejects-eu-aid-again.html

Cockburn, C. (1989). Equal opportunities: The short and long agenda. *Industrial Relations Journal, 20*(3), 213–225. doi:10.1111/j.1468-2338.1989.tb00068.x.

Cockburn, C. (2007). *From where we stand: War, women's activism and feminist analysis*. Zed Books.

Cockburn, C. (2012). Gender relations as causal in militarization and war: A feminist standpoint. In A. Kronsell & B. Svedberg (Eds.), *Making gender, making war: Violence, military and peacekeeping practices* (pp. 19–34). Routledge.

Cohn, C., Kinsella, H., & Gibbings, S. (2004). Women, Peace and Security Resolution 1325. *International Feminist Journal of Politics, 6*(1), 130–140. doi:10.1080/146 1674032000165969.

Commission on the Filipinos Overseas (CFO). (n.d.). *Philippine migration at a glance*. https://cfo.gov.ph/statistics-2

Committee for the Elimination of All Forms of Discrimination against Women (CEDAW). (2013). *General recommendation no. 30 on women in conflict prevention, conflict and post-conflict situations (CEDAW/C/GC/30)*. CEDAW.

Coomarswamy, R. (2015). *A global study on the implementation of United Nations Security Council Resolution 1325*. UN Women.

Council of Australian Governments (COAG). (2011). *The national plan to reduce violence against women and their children*. FaHCSIA.

Crenshaw, K. (1991). Mapping the margins: Intersectionality, identity politics, and violence against women of color. *Stanford Law Review, 43*(6), 1241–1299. doi:10.2307/1229039.

D'Costa, B., & Lee-Koo, K. (2009). *Gender and global politics in the Asia-Pacific*. Palgrave Macmillan.

Davies, M. (2016). Women and development, not gender and politics: Explaining ASEAN's failure to engage with the Women, Peace and Security agenda. *Contemporary Southeast Asia, 38*(1), 106–127. doi:10.1355/cs38-1e.

Davies, S., & Lee-Koo, K. (2018). *The implementation of the Women, Peace and Security (WPS) agenda: ASEAN and the region.* Monash GPS.

Davies, S. E. (2017). Remembering the human in Asia-Pacific human security. *Australian Journal of International Affairs, 71*(1), 16–19. doi:10.1080/10357718.2016.1243224.

Davies, S. E., Nackers, K., & Teitt, S. (2014). Women, Peace and Security as an ASEAN priority. *Australian Journal of International Affairs, 68*(3), 333–355. doi: 10.1080/10357718.2014.902030.

Davies, S. E., & True, J. (2015). Reframing conflict-related sexual and gender-based violence: Bringing gender analysis back in. *Security Dialogue, 46*(6), 495–512. doi:10.1177/0967010615601389.

Davies, S. E., & True, J. (2019). Pitfalls, policy, and promise of the UN's approach to conflict-related sexual violence and the new Resolution 2467. https://blogs.prio.org/2019/05/pitfalls-policy-and-promise-of-the-uns-approach-to-conflict-related-sexual-violence-and-the-new-resolution-2467

Dioniso, J., & Cabrera-Balleza, M. (2009). *Towards full implementation of UNSCR 1325 in the Philippines: Crafting a national action plan for women and peacebuilding.* Manila.

Douglas, S. (2015). "What gets measured gets done": Translating accountability frameworks into better responses for women and girls in peacebuilding contexts. *Journal of Peacebuilding & Development, 10*(1), 90–96. doi:10.1080/15423166.2015.1008888.

Duncanson, C. (2016). *Gender and peacebuilding.* Polity Press.

Duncanson, C., & Woodward, R. (2016). Regendering the military: Theorizing women's military participation. *Security Dialogue, 47*(1), 3–21. doi:10.1177/0967010615614137.

Dunn, M. E. (2014). Localising the Australian National Action Plan on Women, Peace and Security: A matter of justice. *Australian Journal of International Affairs, 68*(3), 285–299. doi:10.1080/10357718.2014.902031.

Egnell, R. (2016). Gender perspectives and military effectiveness: Implementing UNSCR 1325 and the National Action Plan on Women, Peace, and Security. *Prism: A Journal of the Center for Complex Operations, 6*(1), 72–89.

Engle, K. (2005). Feminism and its (dis)contents: Criminalizing wartime rape in Bosnia and Herzegovina. *American Journal of International Law, 99*(4), 778–816. doi:10.2307/3396669.

Enloe, C. (1989). *Bananas, beaches and bases: Making feminist sense of international politics.* University of California Press.

Enloe, C. (2000). *Maneuvers: The international politics of militarizing women's lives.* University of California Press.

Enloe, C. (2004). *The curious feminist: Searching for women in a new age of empire.* University of California Press.

Enloe, C. (2014). *Bananas, beaches and bases: Making feminist sense of international politics.* University of California Press.

FemLINKPACIFIC. (n.d.). *FemLINKPACIFIC: Media initiatives for women.* https://www.femlinkpacific.org.fj.

Flood, M., Dragiewicz, M., & Pease, B. (2020). Resistance and backlash to gender equality. *Australian Journal of Social Issues*, 1–16. doi:10.1002/ajs4.137.

Fritz, J. M., Doering, S., & Gumru, B. (2011). Women, Peace, Security, and the national action plans. *Journal of Applied Social Science, 5*(1), 1–23. doi:10.1177/1936724411100500101.

George, N. (2014). Promoting Women, Peace and Security in the Pacific islands: Hot conflict/slow violence. *Australian Journal of International Affairs, 68*(3), 314–332. doi:10.1080/10357718.2014.902032.

George, N. (2016). Institutionalising Women, Peace and Security in the Pacific islands: Gendering the "architecture of entitlements"? *International Political Science Review, 37*(3), 375–389. doi:10.1177/0192512116629819.

George, N., Lee-Koo, K., & Shepherd, L. J. (2019). Gender and the UN's Women, Peace and Security agenda. In *Routledge handbook of gender and security* (pp. 311–322). Routledge.

Gibbings, S. L. (2011). No angry women at the United Nations: Political dreams and the cultural politics of United Nations Security Council Resolution 1325. *International Feminist Journal of Politics, 13*(4), 522–538. doi:10.1080/14616742.2011.611660.

Gierycz, D. (2001). Women, peace and the United Nations: Beyond Beijing. In I. Skjelsbæk & D. Smith (Eds.), *Gender, peace and conflict* (pp. 14–31). SAGE.

Gizelis, T.-I., & Olsson, L. (2015). *Gender, peace and security: Implementing UN Security Council Resolution 1325*. Routledge.

Global Network of Women Peacebuilders. (2021). *The pandemic will not stop us: The impact of COVID-19 on women's peace activism in Colombia, the Philippines, South Sudan and Ukraine*. Global Network of Women Peacebuilders.

Goetz, A. M. (2016). *Still no woman at the helm of the UN*. https://www.opendemocracy.net/5050/anne-marie-goetz/still-no-woman-at-helm-UN

Goetz, A. M. (2017). *The silencing of Leila de Lima—Duterte's "first political prisoner."* https://www.opendemocracy.net/5050/anne-marie-goetz/silencing-leila-de -lima-philippines

Gordon, E. (2020). *Consequences of the pandemic on conflicts in Asia: Challenges and recommendations*. https://www.monash.edu/arts/gender-peace-security/news -and-events/articles/consequences-of-the-pandemic-on-conflicts-in-asia-challenges-and-recommendations

Government of Australia. (2012). *The Australian National Action Plan on Women, Peace and Security*. Government of Australia.

Government of Australia. (2021). *Australian National Action Plan on Women, Peace and Security*. Government of Australia.

Government of Indonesia. (2014). *National Action Plan for the protection and empowerment of women and children during social conflicts*. Government of Indonesia.

Government of New Zealand. (2015). *New Zealand National Action Plan for the implementation of United Nations Security Council Resolutions, including 1325, on Women, Peace and Security*. Government of New Zealand.

Government of the Philippines. (2010). *The Philippine National Action Plan on UNSCR 1325 and 1820*. Government of the Philippines.

Government of the Philippines. (2014). *The Philippine National Action Plan on UNSCR 1325 and 1820* [refreshed]. Government of the Philippines.

Government of the Philippines. (2017). *National Action Plan on Women, Peace and Security*. Government of the Philippines.

Government of the Solomon Islands. (2017). *Solomon Islands Women, Peace and Security National Action Plan*. Government of the Solomon Islands.

Guardian. (2017). Rodrigo Duterte jokes to soldiers that they can rape women with impunity. https://www.theguardian.com/world/2017/may/27/rodrigo-duterte-jokes -to-soldiers-that-they-can-women-with-impunity

Hagen, J. (2016). Queering Women, Peace and Security. *International Affairs, 92*(2), 313–332. doi:10.1111/1468–2346.12551.

Hall, R. (2012). Modern soldiery interrogated: Cataloguing the local military's tasks and their perception of local civilian actors. *Philippine Political Science Journal, 33*(1), 1–21. doi:10.1080/01154451.2012.684514.

Hall, R. (2016). Unveiled: Narratives from Muslim women in the Philippine army. *Res Militaris, 2*(2), 1–21.

Hall, R. A., & Hoare, J. P. (2015). Philippines. In J. Hedstrom & T. Senarathna (Eds.), *Women in conflict and peace* (pp. 89–122). International IDEA.

Hamilton, C., Naam, N., & Shepherd, L. J. (2020). *Twenty years of Women, Peace and Security national action plans: Analysis and lessons learned*. The University of Sydney.

Hanisch, C. (1969). The personal is political. In S. Firestone & A. Koedt (Eds.), *Notes from the second year: Women's liberation*. Radical Feminism.

Harris Rimmer, S. (2016). Gender, governance and defence of the realm: Globalising reforms in the Australian Defence Force. In K. Young & K. Rubenstein (Eds.), *The public law of gender* (pp. 413–436). Cambridge University Press.

Harris Rimmer, S., & Sawer, M. (2016). Neoliberalism and gender equality policy in Australia. *Australian Journal of Political Science, 51*(4), 742–758. doi:10.1080/1 0361146.2016.1222602.

Hartley, D., Shepherd, L. J., Porter, E., Gildea, A., Hayter, J., Boyd, S., & Davies, G. (2018). *Final independent review of the National Action Plan on Women, Peace and Security 2012–2018*. Department of the Prime Minister and Cabinet.

Heathcote, G., & Otto, D. (2014). *Rethinking peacekeeping, gender equality and collective security*. Palgrave Macmillan.

Hernes, H. (1987). *Welfare state and woman power: Essays in state feminism*. Norwegian University Press.

Hesse-Biber, S. (2012). *Handbook of feminist research: Theory and praxis*. SAGE.

Hewitt, S. (2017). Gender, peace and security in the Australian Defence Force: Sarah Hewitt in conversation with Captain Jennifer Wittwer, CSM, RAN. *International Feminist Journal of Politics, 19*(1), 104–111. doi:10.1080/14616742.2016.1253 242.

Heyzer, N. (2020). *Women, Peace and Security in ASEAN: New issues*. S. Rajaratnam School of International Studies.

Hudson, N. (2009). *Gender, human security and the United Nations: Security language as a political framework for women*. Routledge.

Hudson, N. (2013). *National and regional implementation of Security Council resolutions on Women, Peace and Security*. UN Women.

Human Rights Watch (HRW). (2018). *World report 2018*. HRW.

Human Rights Watch (HRW). (2019). *World report 2019*. HRW.

Human Rights Watch (HRW). (2020). *World report 2020*. HRW.

Human Rights Watch (HRW). (2021). *World report 2021*. HRW.

Humanitarian Advisory Group (HAG). (2015). *Independent interim review of the Australian National Action Plan on Women, Peace and Security 2012–2018*. HAG.

Huvé, S. (2018). *The use of UN sanctions to address conflict-related sexual violence*. Georgetown Institute for Women, Peace and Security.

Jansson, M., & Eduards, M. (2012). Disarming the peace process: A feminist approach to gender and security. In L. Freidenvall & M. Micheletti (Eds.), *Comparisons, quotas and critical change* (pp. 119–134). Stockholm University Press.

Jay, H., Johnson, L., Lee-Koo, K., & Trojanowska, B. K. (2016). *Fourth annual civil society report card: Australia's National Action Plan on Women, Peace and Security*. Monash GPS.

Joachim, J., & Schneiker, A. (2012). Changing discourses, changing practices: Gender mainstreaming and security. *Comparative European Politics, 10*(5), 528–563. doi:10.1057/cep.2011.35.

Kantola, J., & Squires, J. (2010). The new politics of equality. In C. Hay (Ed.), *New directions in political science: Responding to the challenges of an interdependent world* (pp. 88–108). Palgrave Macmillan.

Kardam, N. (2004). The emerging global gender equality regime from neoliberal and constructivist perspectives in international relations. *International Feminist Journal of Politics, 6*(1), 85–109. doi:10.1080/1461674032000165941.

Kholifah, R. (2014). *Indonesian implementation of UNSCR 1325: Adapting to the national context*. https://womenpeacemakersprogram.org/news/indonesian-implementation-of-unscr-1325-adapting-to-the-national-context

Kirby, P., & Shepherd, L. J. (2016). The futures past of the Women, Peace and Security agenda. *International Affairs, 92*(2), 373–392. doi:10.1111/1468–2346.12549.

Koens, C., & Gunawardana, S. J. (2020). A continuum of participation: Rethinking Tamil women's political participation and agency in post-war Sri Lanka. *International Feminist Journal of Politics*, 1–22. doi:10.1080/1461674032000165941.

Krizsan, A., Skjeie, H., & Squires, J. (2014). The changing nature of European equality regimes: Explaining convergence and variation. *Journal of International and Comparative Social Policy, 30*(1), 53–68. doi:10.1080/21699763.2014.886612.

Kronsell, A., & Svedberg, E. (2011). *Making gender, making war: Violence, military and peacekeeping practices*. Routledge.

Krook, M. L. (2006). Reforming representation: The diffusion of candidate gender quotas worldwide. *Politics & Gender, 2*(3), 303–327. doi:10.1017/S1743923X06060107.

Krook, M. L., & True, J. (2012). Rethinking the life cycles of international norms: The United Nations and the global promotion of gender equality. *European Journal of International Relations, 18*(1), 103–127. doi:10.1177/1354066110380963.

Lee-Koo, K. (2012). Gender at the crossroad of conflict: Tsunami and peace in post-2005 Aceh. *Feminist Review, 101*(1), 59–77. doi:10.1057/fr.2011.54.

Lee-Koo, K. (2014). Implementing Australia's National Action Plan on United Nations Security Council Resolution 1325. *Australian Journal of International Affairs, 68*(3), 300–313. doi:10.1080/10357718.2014.901296.

Lee-Koo, K. (2016). Engaging UNSCR 1325 through Australia's National Action Plan. *International Political Science Review, 37*(3), 336–349. doi:10.1177/0192512116629821.

Lee-Koo, K. (2017). Feminism. In R. Devetak, J. George, & S. Percy (Eds.), *An introduction to international relations* (pp. 78–93). Cambridge University Press.

Lee-Koo, K. (2018). *Connecting displacement and the WPS agenda.* https://www.aspistrategist.org.au/wps-2018-connecting-displacement-wps-agenda

Lee-Koo, K., & Trojanowska, B. K. (2017). Does the United Nations' Women, Peace and Security agenda speak with, for or to women in the Asia Pacific? The development of national action plans in the Asia Pacific. *Critical Studies on Security, 5*(3), 287–301. doi:10.1080/21624887.2017.1411667.

Lewis, C. (2014). Systemic silencing: Addressing sexual violence against men and boys in armed conflict and its aftermath. In G. Heathcote & D. Otto (Eds.), *Rethinking peacekeeping, gender equality and collective security* (pp. 203–223). Routledge.

Lombardo, E., Meier, P., & Verloo, M. (2009). *The discursive politics of gender equality: Stretching, bending and policy-making.* London and Routledge.

Lombardo, E., Meier, P., & Verloo, M. (2010). Discursive dynamics in gender equality politics: What about "feminist taboos"? *European Journal of Women's Studies, 17*(2), 105–123. doi:10.1177/1350506809359562.

London School of Economics (LSE) & University of Sydney (USYD). (n.d.). *WPS national action plans.* https://www.wpsnaps.org

MacKenzie, M. (2012). Let women fight: Ending the US military's female combat ban. *Foreign Affairs, 91*(6), 32–42.

MacKinnon, C. (2013). Intersectionality as method: A note. *Signs: Journal of Women in Culture and Society, 38*(4), 1019–1030. doi:10.1086/669570.

McCall, L. (2005). The complexity of intersectionality. *Signs: Journal of Women in Culture and Society, 30*(3), 1771-1800. doi:10.1086/426800.

McDonald, M. (2017). Critical security in the Asia-Pacific: An introduction. *Critical Studies on Security, 5*(3), 237–252.

Miller, B., Pournik, M., & Swaine, A. (2014). *Women in peace and security through United Nations Security Resolution 1325: Literature review, content analysis of national action plans, and implementation.* Georgetown Institute for Women, Peace and Security.

Monash Gender Peace and Security. (2021). *Analyses of Australia's second national action plan (NAP) on Women, Peace and Security (WPS) 2021–2032.* Monash GPS.

Mundkur, A., & Shepherd, L. J. (2018). Civil society participation in Women, Peace and Security governance: Insights from Australia. *Security Challenges, 14*(2), 84–105.

Nair, T. (2018). *Upscaling disaster resilience in Southeast Asia: Engaging women through the WPS agenda*. S. Rajaratnam School of International Studies.

Nario-Galace, J., & Piscano, Y. (2010). *Women count: Security Council Resolution 1325. The Philippines*. Global Network of Women Peacebuilders.

Nario-Galace, J., & Piscano, Y. (2011). *Women count: Security Council Resolution 1325. The Philippines*. Global Network of Women Peacebuilders.

Nasu, H. (2011). Introduction: Regional integration and human rights monitoring institutions. In H. Nasu & B. Saul (Eds.), *Human rights in the Asia-Pacific region: Towards institution building* (pp. 1–14). Routledge.

Natividad, A. M., Piscano, Y., & Viar, I. (2013). *Women count: Security Council Resolution 1325. The Philippines*. Global Network of Women Peacebuilders.

Ní Aoláin, F. (2016). The "war on terror" and extremism: Assessing the relevance of the Women, Peace and Security agenda. *International Affairs, 92*(2), 275–291. doi:10.1111/1468-2346.12552.

Nobel Women's Initiative. (2014). *Women lead Philippines historic peace accord*. https://nobelwomensinitiative.org/women-lead-philippines-in-historic-peace-accord

O'Rourke, C. (2014). Walk[ing] the halls of power: Understanding women's participation in international peace and security. *Melbourne Journal of International Law, 15*(1), 1–27.

Office of the United Nations High Commissioner for Human Rights (OHCHR). (2019). *UN human rights experts call for independent probe into Philippines violations*. https://www.ohchr.org/EN/NewsEvents/Pages/DisplayNews.aspx?NewsID=24679&LangID=E

Organisation for Economic Co-operation and Development (OECD). (2021). *Official development assistance*. https://www.oecd.org/dac/financing-sustainable-development/development-finance-standards/official-development-assistance.htm

Østebø, M. (2015). Translations of gender equality among rural Arsi Oromo in Ethiopia. *Development and Change, 46*(3), 442–463. doi:10.1111/dech.12159.

Østebø, M., & Haukanes, H. (2016). Shifting meanings of gender equality in development: Perspectives from Norway and Ethiopia. *Progress in Development Studies, 16*(1), 39–51. doi:10.1177/1464993415608081.

Otto, D. (2010). The Security Council's alliance of gender legitimacy: The symbolic capital of Resolution 1325. In H. Charlesworth & J. Coicaud (Eds.), *Fault lines of international legitimacy* (pp. 239–278). Cambridge University Press.

Otto, D., & Heathcote, G. (2014). Rethinking peacekeeping, gender equality and collective security: An introduction. In G. Heathcote & D. Otto (Eds.), *Rethinking peacekeeping, gender equality and collective security* (pp. 1–22). Palgrave Macmillan.

Pacific Islands Forum (PIF). (2000). *Biketawa Declaration*. PIF.

Pacific Islands Forum (PIF). (2012). *Pacific Regional Action Plan: Women, Peace and Security*. PIF.

Pacific Islands Forum (PIF). (2018). *The Boe Declaration of Regional Security*. PIF.

Pacific Islands Forum (PIF). (n.d.). *Mission and vision*. http://www.forumsec.org/pages.cfm/about-us/mission-goals-roles

Parashar, S. (2018). The WPS agenda: A postcolonial critique. In *The Oxford handbook of Women, Peace, and Security* (pp. 829–839). Oxford University Press.

PeaceWomen. (2021). *Member states.* https://www.peacewomen.org/member-states

Phelan, A. (2020). Special issue introduction for terrorism, gender and women: Toward an integrated research agenda. *Studies in Conflict & Terrorism, April 2020.* doi:10.1080/1057610X.2020.1759252.

Philippine Commission on Women (PCW). (2009). *Republic Act 9710: Magna Carta of Women.* Government of the Philippines.

Philippine Commission on Women (PCW). (n.d.). *Republic Act 9710: Magna Carta of women.* https://pcw.gov.ph/republic-act-9710-magna-carta-of-women/.

Philippine Government Office of the Presidential Adviser on the Peace Process (OPAPP). (2016a). *National Action Plan on Women, Peace and Security: The Philippines experience.* Government of the Philippines.

Philippine Government Office of the Presidential Adviser on the Peace Process (OPAPP). (2016b). *Women, Peace and Security: A study of the initiatives to implement United Nations Resolution 1325.* Government of the Philippines.

Philippine Government Office of the Presidential Adviser on the Peace Process (OPAPP). (2020). *Peace Tables.* https://peace.gov.ph/peace-tables

Philippine Government Office of the Presidential Adviser on the Peace Process (OPAPP), & Philippine Commission on Women (PCW). (2014). *Joint memorandum circular no. 2014-01: Integration of Women, Peace and Security programs, activities and projects (PAPs) in annual Gender and Development (GAD) plans and budgets (GPBs) and Gender and Development accomplishments reports (GAD ARs).* Government of the Philippines.

Phillips, A. (1999). *Which equalities matter?* Polity Press.

Phillips, A. (2004). Defending equality of outcome. *Journal of Political Philosophy, 12*(1), 1–19.

Piscano, Y., Raine Au, B., Martinez, L. M., Enriquez, E., & Talon, V. (2012). *Women count: Security Council Resolution 1325. The Philippines.* Global Network of Women Peacebuilders.

Porter, E. (2009). *Final report: Developing a national action plan on United Nations Security Council Resolution 1325.* WILPF.

Pratt, N. (2013). Reconceptualizing gender, reinscribing racial-sexual boundaries in international security: The case of UN Security Council Resolution 1325 on "Women, Peace and Security." *International Studies Quarterly, 57*(4), 772–783. doi:10.1111/isqu.12032.

Prescott, J. M., Iwata, E., & Pincus, B. H. (2015). Gender, law and policy: Japan's National Action Plan on Women, Peace and Security. *Asian-Pacific Law & Policy Journal, 17*(1), 1–45.

President of the Philippines. (2010). *Executive order no. 865: Creating of a national steering committee on Women, Peace and Security to implement the UN Security Council Resolutions 1325 and 1820 and providing funds thereof.* Government of the Philippines.

President of the Philippines. (2011). *National Security Policy 2011–2016: Securing the gains of democracy.* Government of the Philippines.

President of the Philippines. (2017). *National Security Policy 2017–2022: Change and well-being of the Filipino people.* Government of the Philippines.

Rajan, G., & Desai, J. (2013). Transnational feminism and global advocacy in South Asia. In G. Rajan & J. Desai (Eds.), *Transnational feminism and global advocacy in South Asia.* Routledge.

Renshaw, C. (2017). Global or regional? Realizing women's rights in Southeast Asia. *Human Rights Quarterly, 39*(3), 707–745. doi:10.1353/hrq.2017.0038.

Reuters. (2017). *UN says "massive" rights abuses in southern Philippines could intensify under Martial Law.* http://www.reuters.com/article/us-philippines-security/u-n-says-massive-rights-abuses-in-southern-philippines-could-intensify-under -martial-law-idUSKBN1EM0SN

Ruby, F. (2014). Security Council Resolution 1325: A tool for conflict prevention? In G. Heathcote & D. Otto (Eds.), *Rethinking peacekeeping, gender equality and collective security* (pp. 173–184). Palgrave Macmillan.

Shaw, C., Mundkur, A., & Cooper, M. (2010). *Women organizing for an Australian National Action Plan on Security Council Resolution 1325.* WILPF.

Shepherd, L. J. (2017). The Women, Peace, and Security agenda at the United Nations. In A. Burke & R. Parker (Eds.), *Global insecurity* (pp. 139–158). Palgrave Macmillan.

Shepherd, L. J. (2014). *Advancing the Women, Peace and Security agenda: 2015 and beyond.* NOREF.

Shepherd, L. J. (2016). Making war safe for women? National action plans and the militarisation of the Women, Peace and Security agenda. *International Political Science Review, 37*(3), 324–335. doi:10.1177/0192512116629820.

Shepherd, L. J., & True, J. (2014). The Women, Peace and Security agenda and Australian leadership in the world: From rhetoric to commitment? *Australian Journal of International Affairs, 68*(3), 257–284. doi:10.1080/10357718.2014.90 3895.

Simić, O. (2010). Does the presence of women really matter? Towards combating male sexual violence in peacekeeping operations. *International Peacekeeping, 17*(2), 188–199.

Sivakumaran, S. (2007). Sexual violence against men in armed conflict. *European Journal of International Law, 18*(2), 253–276.

Skjeie, H., & Teigen, M. (2005). Political constructions of gender equality: Travelling towards a gender balanced society? *NORA: Nordic Journal of Women's Studies, 13*(3), 187–197. doi:10.1080/08038740600590004.

Sloane, J. (2017). *Toward a regional action plan on Women, Peace, and Security in Asia.* https://asiafoundation.org/2017/07/12/toward-regional-action-plan-women -peace-security-asia

Squires, J. (2007). *The new politics of gender equality.* Palgrave Macmillan.

Squires, J. (2013). *Gender in political theory.* Polity Press.

Swaine, A. (2009). Assessing the potential of national action plans to advance implementation of United Nations Security Council Resolution 1325. *Yearbook of International Humanitarian Law, 12*, 403–433. doi:10.1017/S1389135909000142.

Swaine, A. (2013). *National implementation of the UN Security Council's Women, Peace and Security resolutions.* NOREF.

Swaine, A. (2016). Making women's and girl's needs, well-being and rights central to national action plans in the Asia-Pacific region. UN Women.

Swaine, A. (2017). Globalising Women, Peace and Security: Trends in national action plans. In S. Aroussi (Ed.), *Rethinking national action plans on Women, Peace and Security* (pp. 7–27). IOS Press.

Swaine, A., & O'Rourke, C. (2015). *Guidebook on CEDAW general recommendation no. 30 and the UN Security Council resolutions on Women, Peace and Security.* UN Women.

Tanyag, M. (2018). *Hypermasculinity and the key to populism.* http://www.internationalaffairs.org.au/australianoutlook/duterte-governing-hypermasculinity-philippines

Tickner, J. A. (1992). *Gender in international relations: Feminist perspectives on achieving global security.* Columbia University Press.

Tickner, J. A. (1997). You just don't understand: Troubled engagements between feminists and IR theorists. *International Studies Quarterly, 41*(4), 611–632. doi:10.1111/1468-2478.00060.

Tickner, J. A. (2010). You may never understand: Prospects for feminist futures in international relations. *Australian Feminist Law Journal, 32*(1), 9–20. doi:10.1080/13200968.2010.10854434.

Tickner, J. A., & Sjoberg, L. (2013). *Feminism and international relations: Conversations about the past, present and future.* Routledge.

Tickner, J. A., & True, J. (2018). A century of international relations feminism: From World War I women's peace pragmatism to the Women, Peace and Security agenda. *International Studies Quarterly, 62*(2), 221–233. doi:10.1093/isq/sqx091.

Trisko Darden, J. (2015). Assessing the significance of women in combat roles. *Canada's Journal of Global Policy Analysis, 70*(3), 454–462. doi:10.1177/0020702015585306.

Trojanowska, B. K. (2019). Norm negotiation in the Australian government's implementation of UNSCR 1325. *Australian Journal of International Affairs, 73*(1), 29–44. doi:10.1080/10357718.2018.1548560.

Trojanowska, B. K. (2021). Women's rights facing hypermasculinist leadership: Implementing the Women, Peace and Security agenda under a populist-nationalist regime. *Feminist Legal Studies, 29*(2), 231–249. doi:10.1007/s10691-021-09464-4.

Trojanowska, B. K., Lee-Koo, K., & Johnson, L. (2018). *National action plans on Women, Peace and Security: Eight countries in focus.* Australian Civil-Military Centre.

True, J. (2003). Mainstreaming gender in global public policy. *International Feminist Journal of Politics, 5*(3), 368–396. doi:10.1080/1461674032000122740.

True, J. (2010). Mainstreaming gender in global public policy. *International Feminist Journal of Politics, 5*(3), 368–396. doi:10.1080/1461674032000122740.

True, J. (2016). Explaining the global diffusion of the Women, Peace and Security agenda. *International Political Science Review, 37*(3), 307–323. doi:10.1177/0192512116632372

True, J., & Eddyono, S. W. (2017). *Preventing violent extremism: Gender perspectives and women's roles.* Monash GPS.

True, J., & Mintrom, M. (2001). Transnational networks and policy diffusion: The case of gender mainstreaming. *International Studies Quarterly, 45*(1), 27–57. doi:10.1111/0020-8833.00181.

True, J., & Parisi, L. (2013). Gender mainstreaming strategies in international governance. In G. Caglar, E. Prugl, & S. Zwingel (Eds.), *Feminist strategies in international governance* (pp. 37–56). Routledge.

True, J., & Wiener, A. (2019). Everyone wants (a) peace: The dynamics of rhetoric and practice on "Women, Peace and Security." *International Affairs, 95*(3), 553–574. doi:10.1093/ia/iiz027.

Tryggestad, T. (2009). Trick or treat? The UN and implementation of Security Council Resolution 1325 on Women, Peace, and Security. *Global Governance, 15*(4), 539–557. doi:10.1163/19426720-01504011.

Tryggestad, T. (2014). *International norms and political change: Women, Peace and Security and the UN security agenda* [Unpublished doctoral dissertation]. University of Oslo.

United Nations (UN). (1945). *Charter of the United Nations.* UN.

United Nations (UN). (2005). *Responsibility to protect.* https://www.un.org/en/genocideprevention/about-responsibility-to-protect.shtml

United Nations (UN). (2020). *Guterres to Security Council: Women leaders "essential to peace and progress for all."* https://news.un.org/en/story/2020/10/1076462

United Nations Department of Peace Operations (UNDPO). (2021). *Troop and police contributors.* https://peacekeeping.un.org/en/troop-and-police-contributors

United Nations Development Programme (UNDP). (2021). *Women's Peace and Humanitarian Fund.* http://mptf.undp.org/factsheet/fund/GAI00

United Nations Diplomatic Conference. (1988). *Rome Statute of the International Criminal Court (A/CONF.183/9).* United Nations Diplomatic Conference.

United Nations Economic and Social Council (ECOSOC). (1988). *Agreed conclusions of the 42nd Commission on the Status of Women (E/1998/INF/3/Add.2).* ECOSOC.

United Nations Economic and Social Council (ECOSOC). (1988). *Report of the Commission on the Status of Women to the Economic and Social Council (E/281/REV.1).* ECOSOC.

United Nations Entity for Gender Equality (UN Women). (2018). *Strategic plan 2018–2021 (UNW/2017/6/Rev.1).* UN Women.

United Nations Entity for Gender Equality (UN Women). (n.d.). *The shadow pandemic: Violence against women during COVID-19.* https://www.unwomen.org/en/news/in-focus/in-focus-gender-equality-in-covid-19-response/violence-against-women-during-covid-19

United Nations General Assembly (UNGA). (1985). *The Nairobi forward-looking strategies for the advancement of women.* UNGA.

United Nations General Assembly (UNGA). (1995). *Beijing declaration and platform for action.* UNGA.

United Nations Refugee Agency (UNHCR). (2020). Mindanao displacement dashboard. https://reliefweb.int/sites/reliefweb.int/files/resources/Mindanao-Displacement -Dashboard_-APR2020–2.pdf

United Nations Security Council (UNSC). (2000a). *Peace inextricably linked with equality between women and men says Security Council in International Women's Day statement. Press release (SC/6816).* UNSC.

United Nations Security Council (UNSC). (2000b). *Resolution 1325 (S/RES/1325).* UNSC.

United Nations Security Council (UNSC). (2000c). *Windhoek Declaration and the Namibia plan of action on mainstreaming a gender perspective in multidimensional peace support operations (S/2000/693).* UNSC.

United Nations Security Council (UNSC). (2002a). *Report of the secretary-general on Women, Peace and Security (S/2002/1154).* UNSC.

United Nations Security Council (UNSC). (2002b). *Statement by the president of the Security Council (S/PRST/2002/32).* UNSC.

United Nations Security Council (UNSC). (2004). *Report of the secretary-general on Women, Peace and Security (S/2004/814).* UNSC.

United Nations Security Council (UNSC). (2005). *Report of the secretary-general on Women, Peace and Security (S/2005/636).* UNSC.

United Nations Security Council (UNSC). (2008). *Resolution 1820 (S/RES/1820).* UNSC.

United Nations Security Council (UNSC). (2009a). *Resolution 1888 (S/RES/1888).* UNSC.

United Nations Security Council (UNSC). (2009b). *Resolution 1889 (S/RES/1889).* UNSC.

United Nations Security Council (UNSC). (2010a). *Resolution 1960 (S/RES/1960).* UNSC.

United Nations Security Council (UNSC). (2010b). *Report of the secretary-general on women's participation in peacebuilding (A/65/354-S/2010/466).* UNSC.

United Nations Security Council (UNSC). (2013a). *Resolution 2106 (S/RES/2106).* UNSC.

United Nations Security Council (UNSC). (2013b). *Resolution 2122 (S/RES/2122).* UNSC.

United Nations Security Council (UNSC). (2013c). *Resolution 2177 (S/RES/2177).* UNSC.

United Nations Security Council (UNSC). (2014). *Resolution 2145 (S/RES/2145).* UNSC.

United Nations Security Council (UNSC). (2015a). *Meeting record (S/PV.7533).* UNSC.

United Nations Security Council (UNSC). (2015b). *Resolution 2242 (S/RES/2242).* UNSC.

United Nations Security Council (UNSC). (2016). *Guidelines for the informal group on Women, Peace and Security (S/2016/1106).* UNSC.

United Nations Security Council (UNSC). (2018a). *Meeting record (S/PV.8382).* UNSC.

United Nations Security Council (UNSC). (2018b). *Report of the secretary-general on Women, Peace and Security (S/2018/900)*. UNSC.

United Nations Security Council (UNSC). (2019a). *Meeting record (S/PV.8514)*. UNSC.

United Nations Security Council (UNSC). (2019b). *Meeting record (S/PV.8649)*. UNSC.

United Nations Security Council (UNSC). (2019c). *Resolution 2467 (S/RES/2467)*. UNSC.

United Nations Security Council (UNSC). (2019d). *Resolution 2493 (S/RES/2493)*. UNSC.

United Nations Security Council (UNSC). (2020a). *Letter dated 30 October 2020 from the president of the Security Council addressed to the secretary-general and the permanent representatives of the members of the Security Council (S/2020/1076)*. UNSC.

United Nations Security Council (UNSC). (2020b). *Report of the secretary-general on Women, Peace and Security (S/2020/946)*. UNSC.

United Nations Security Council (UNSC). (2020c). *Resolution 2538 (S/RES/2538)*. UNSC.

United Nations Security Council (UNSC). (2020d). *United Nations cooperation with South-East Asian Nations Association vital for fight against climate change, terrorism, Organizations' Chiefs tells Security Council (SC/14093)*. UNSC.

Uppsala Conflict Data Program (UCDP). (n.d.a). *Philippines*. https://ucdp.uu.se/country/840

Uppsala Conflict Data Program (UCDP). (n.d.b). *Uppsala conflict data program*. https://ucdp.uu.se

Valenius, J. (2007). A few kind women: Gender essentialism and Nordic peacekeeping operations. *International Peacekeeping, 14*(4), 510–523. doi:10.1080/13533310701427785.

Veneracion-Rallonza, L. (2013). Grounding the international norm on Women, Peace and Security: The role of domestic norm entrepreneurs and the challenges ahead. *Femina Politica-Zeitschrift für feministische Politikwissenschaft, 22*(2), 67–85.

Veneracion-Rallonza, L. (2014). *National Action Plan ensures protection, spaces for Women, Peace and Security*. KABABAIHANatKAPAYAPAAN.

Veneracion-Rallonza, L., & Rallonza, M. (2014). *Women count: Security Council Resolution 1325. The Philippines*. Global Network of Women Peacebuilders.

Veneracion-Rallonza, L. (2019). WPS and the Association of South East Asian Nations. In *The Oxford handbook of Women, Peace and Security* (pp. 388–401). Oxford University Press.

Verloo, M. (2018). Understanding the dynamics of opposition to gender equality change: Lessons from and for social complexity theory. In M. Verloo (Ed.), *Varieties of opposition to gender equality in Europe* (pp. 38–54). Routledge.

Walby, S. (2005). Gender mainstreaming: Productive tensions in theory and practice. *Social Politics: International Studies in Gender, State & Society, 12*(3), 321–343. doi:10.1093/sp/jxi018.

Walby, S., Armstrong, J., & Strid, S. (2012). Intersectionality and the quality of the gender equality architecture. *Social Politics, 19*(4), 446–481. doi:10.1093/sp/jxs015.

Westendorf, J.-K. (2013). "Add women and stir": The Regional Assistance Mission to Solomon Islands and Australia's implementation of United Nations Security Council Resolution 1325. *Australian Journal of International Affairs, 67*(4), 456–474. doi:10.1080/10357718.2013.803030.

Westendorf, J.-K., & Searle, L. (2017). Sexual exploitation and abuse in peace operations: Trends, policy responses and future directions. *International Affairs, 93*(2), 365–387. doi:10.1093/ia/iix001.

What's in Blue. (2019). *In hindsight: Negotiations on Resolution 2467 on Sexual Violence in Conflict.* https://www.whatsinblue.org/2019/05/in-hindsight-negotiations-on-resolution-2467-on-sexual-violence-in-conflict.php#

Whooley, J., & Sjoberg, L. (2019). *Feminist curiosity as method.* SAGE.

Willett, S. (2010). Introduction: Security Council Resolution 1325. Assessing the impact on Women, Peace and Security. *International Peacekeeping, 17*(2), 142–158. doi:10.1080/13533311003625043.

Women Engaged in Action on UNSCR 1325 (WE Act 1325), & Global Network of Women Peacebuilders (GNWP). (2017). *Localizing the National Action Plan on Women, Peace and Security: The Philippine experience.* GNWP.

World Economic Forum (WEF). (2020). *The Global Gender Gap Report 2020.* WEF.

World Economic Forum (WEF). (2021). *The Global Gender Gap Report 2021.* WEF.

World Economic Forum (WEF). (n.d.). *Reports.* https://www.weforum.org/reports

Young, I. M. (2003). The logic of masculinist protection: Reflections on the current security state. *Signs: Journal of Women in Culture and Society, 29*(1), 1–25. doi:10.1086/375708.

Yuval-Davis, N. (2006). Intersectionality and feminist politics. *European Journal of Women's Studies, 13*(3), 193–209. doi:10.1177/1350506806065752.

Zarkov, D. (2007). *The body of war: Media, ethnicity, and gender in the break-up of Yugoslavia.* Duke University Press.

Zwingel, S., Prugl, E., & Caglar, G. (2014). Feminism. In T. Weiss (Ed.), *International organization and global governance* (pp. 180–191). Routledge.

Index

About the Author

Barbara K. Trojanowska is a researcher, practitioner, and women's rights advocate. Her research and policy interests lie at the intersection of women's rights instruments, global security, and contentious politics. She has published award-winning scholarship as well as reports for government agencies and not-for-profit organizations.

www.ingramcontent.com/pod-product-compliance
Lightning Source LLC
Chambersburg PA
CBHW021819270326
41932CB00007B/251